Unlocked

Keys to Improve Your Thinking

Gerald Zaltman
Harvard Business School

Praise from Others

Jerry Zaltman, master thinker, professor, and writer, once again delivers; here with an engaging, lucid, and scientifically grounded perspective on how we think, why we think the way we do, and how we can improve our thinking. A must-read for even the most thoughtful among us.

Deborah MacInnis, Charles L. and Ramona I. Hilliard Professor of Business Administration, Marshall School of Business, University of Southern California

When my mother would scold me, saying 'If you could take your brain out, would you play with it?' I always thought, 'Yes!' Thanks to the Think Keys in this book, now we can all unlock our thoughts and play with them.

Nancy Cox, market research manager, Hallmark Cards

A highly insightful and extremely engaging book on how we think. Unlocked *provides enjoyable and thought-provoking exercises for us to understand who we are and why we think the way we do. Zaltman is not only a brilliant scientist but also a brilliant storyteller.*

Jagdish Sheth, Charles H. Kellstadt Professor of Business, Emory University

This is truly an amazing book! A reader-friendly brain workout in curiosity. It helps you explore how you think, but also how your loved ones think. My five-year-old said it was 'freakin' fantastic.' In a rushing world, this book is like a breath for the brain.

Jennifer Barba, CEO, Frame Consulting, Mexico

Unlocked *offers a masterful and insightful perspective, guaranteed to change how you and future generations will think.*

Lewis Carbone, CEO and founder of Experience Engineering, and author of *Clued In: How to Bring Customers Back Again and Again*

Zaltman's new book is both serious and fun. He has put together an excellent collection of Think Keys designed to help all of us think more clearly and carefully. I ended up spending the whole evening enjoying the exercises and wanting to tell my friends and family about the book.

Philip Kotler, S. C. Johnson & Son Distinguished Professor of International Marketing, Kellogg School of Management, Northwestern University

Praise from Others (continued)

Practical, simple, thoughtful, and thought provoking, Unlocked *is the perfect guide for modern marketers. And at a time when objective and independent thought and debate is under threat,* Unlocked *is a must-read for young people looking to make sense of the world around them so they can make a positive impact on it.*

David Timm, international marketer and global chief marketing officer, Yum! Brands

I first met Jerry Zaltman when I attended his classes on a Nieman Fellowship at Harvard. I was fascinated and inspired by his insights. I've worked in over 90 countries and covered most of the major world news stories of the past four decades. Rarely have I met someone who always offers a new way to think about a common situation. With Unlocked, *he helps us better understand our personal story and the excitement of living our story well.*

Peter Turnley, Paris-based photojournalist and author of *Cuba: A Grace of Spirit*

I've known and learned from Jerry Zaltman for nearly 40 years. In this book he has clearly 'unlocked' everything he has learned, taught, and consulted on into a form that will be of value to anyone wanting to improve how they listen, learn, and lead.

Vincent Barabba, Market Insight Corporation

Society has drummed into us the need for physical exercise. But there is also a real need to stretch and strengthen our mind. Now, with Jerry Zaltman's fun and engaging mental challenges, he has made exercising our mind easy.

Anne Thistleton, mind science practitioner, Light, Inc., South Africa

Life's journey oftentimes involves a loss of the innocence of childhood. This book is about reengaging your inner child and reawakening curiosity. The 'Think Keys' are playful in intent and compellingly engaging. A must-read for children of all ages—especially adults.

Rohit Deshpande, Sebastian S. Kresge Professor of Marketing, Harvard Business School

Unlocked *is a must-read. The stories are well told, with practical applications and the skills to unlock your mind to a new world of possibilities and more meaningful relationships.*

Gayle Fuguitt, chief of customer insight and innovation, Foursquare, and former CEO and president, the Advertising Research Foundation

Praise from Others (continued)

Curiosity may have killed the cat ... but Zaltman's thought-provoking, fun, 'brain-on' exercises unlock our thinking and engage our curiosity. The incisive mental experiences and their scientific underpinnings aptly illustrate the interplay between the conscious and the unconscious. The book enables us to be aware of, embrace, and play with thinking.

Robin Coulter, University of Connecticut School of Business

Unlocked is an exciting invitation to expand one's realm of perception and thinking. By investigating the Think Keys, one can open the possibility for ever-expanding awareness and creativity. It is about understanding your current constructs so that you can expand your mind to create new possibilities. This is a fun and valuable inquiry tool that educators would be wise to utilize to help expand young minds for a creative and adaptive future.

Sarah Bradley Prindiville, neurodevelopmental educator and school board member, Rockport, ME

Zaltman offers quick, smart ways to start thinking more deeply and wisely as well as wise ways to make smarter decisions in everyday situations. Unlocked provides a guide for educators to inspire, activate, and ensure open and powerful thinking by their students.

John Tielman, senior lecturer on business administration and head of the Curriculum Committee, Inholland University of Applied Sciences

Jerry Zaltman's Unlocked is a must-have element for the tool kit of the new generation of youth leaders and community organizers pressing for urgent and systemic change. Zaltman, a consummate teacher—and an expert in understanding the mental models that undergird human behavior—distills evidence-based prescriptions from behavioral economics and the social sciences to enable aspiring leaders to address the needs and hopes of the communities they seek to serve. With evocative examples and compelling exercises, leaders can also use Unlocked to develop their teams and enhance their ability to make progress on the ground.

Kimberlyn Leary, professor, Harvard Medical School and the Harvard T.H. Chan School of Public Health

Other Books by Gerald Zaltman

Marketing: Contributions from the Behavioral Sciences

Creating Social Change

Processes and Phenomena of Social Change

Innovations and Organizations

Metatheory and Consumer Research

Marketing, Society, and Conflict

Broadening the Concept of Consumer Behavior

Marketing Research: Fundamentals and Dynamics

Cases in Marketing Research

Strategies for Planned Change

Dynamic Educational Change

Review of Marketing

Organizational Buying Behavior

Management Principles for Nonprofit Organizations

Psychology for Managers

Theory Construction in Marketing

Consumer Behavior: Basic Findings and Management Implications

Readings in Consumer Behavior

Marketing Management

Hearing the Voice of the Market

How Customers Think

Marketing Metaphoria

Copyright

This Book is Dedicated to

Sam and Lily Zaltman and Tyler, Brandon, Jared, and Brooke Daniels

The next generation of leaders

Table of Contents

PART I

Introduction

Preface

Today's world is complex, and undergoing rapid and often significant change. We are swimming in information about every issue conceivable, and yet that information is often incomplete and less than reliable. Furthermore, we seem to have less and less time to reflect on information before having to act upon it. And those actions and the beliefs, attitudes, opinions, and experiences underlying them have grown more and more diverse.

More abundant information and more rapid and diverse responses to it are not a bad thing: technological complexity, change, and social diversity add richness to our lives. Increased specialization in the social and natural sciences and the humanities fuels imagination and innovation, the wellsprings of progress. But people can react negatively to complexity and to rapid social and scientific change—for example, by retreating into rigid, deeply entrenched thinking, which leads to diminished curiosity and intolerance of those who think and act differently. Still more worrisome is an unconscious, invisible reluctance to challenge our own thoughts and feelings. Thinking, it seems, is far too often employed to justify an existing position rather than to explore, improve, and perhaps change it.

And those tendencies trouble me. As I watch my grandkids mature into adulthood, I worry about their generation's preparedness for being responsible citizens. They are quite capable of defending their thinking; I don't worry about that. But can they look inward at their thinking, critically examine what they discover, and contemplate making changes? I can't imagine a more important talent or capacity to have today and as we move forward in this century.

So, a couple of years ago I embarked on an effort to equip the teens in my family to be more curious about their minds and how they think. To be clear, my grandchildren are sensitive, inquisitive, reflective young adults. They have dedicated, aware parents and teachers who do the heavy lifting in nurturing their minds. I simply wanted to add a little oomph or push rooted in my experience; a little healthy meddling, as it were.

I approached my task in two ways. One involved preparing written exercises like those in this book. I got some pushback of the "we already have enough homework" sort, but this diminished as my grandchildren gave the exercises a try. The topics turned out to be engaging, and their parents discovered it was fun to make an exercise a discussion topic at dinner. The other approach was to weave a puzzle, dilemma, or thought experiment into a conversation. For instance, if the topic was baseball I might raise the topic of unconscious thinking by asking if a ball is much closer to the pitcher or to the batter when the batter decides to swing at a pitch. (Answer: the pitcher.) Or, I might ask whether "keep your eyes on the ball" is practical advice for a batter. (Answer: not really. Swing mechanics are unconsciously set when the decision to swing is made.) Of course, I would be sure to relate the apparent digression to our conversation.

Over time, friends and colleagues became aware of my undertaking and began using the exercises with their families, friends, and colleagues. As they did, they invariably encouraged me to find a way to share them with people of all ages and from all walks of life. *Unlocked* is a response to this encouragement. It is an invitation to you to learn more about your own and others' thinking. You'll encounter many surprises. Those discoveries are a precious gift you owe to yourself and those you care about. How we think is, after all, the primary driver of the quality of our thoughts.

On balance, I am optimistic that society can learn to place more value on and give more attention to how we think. However, it is not a small task. I am reminded of a meeting my wife and I had with Mother Teresa many years ago. My wife asked Mother Teresa if she wasn't overwhelmed by the numbers of people she was trying to help. Mother Teresa responded, "I start with the one that is before me." *Unlocked* is not an effort to improve how everyone thinks. Just you. Let's start by making a pact between us. You'll find the pact in Chapter One.

Let's Make a Pact

The exercises in the pages ahead offer insight into how you think. Called "Think Keys,*" these brief exercises offer you a chance to observe and inspect your unconscious and conscious ways of thinking. This is sometimes called metacognition. It is step one in learning to think better. Thinking better leads to knowing yourself better, and when you combine those two things, you have a foundation from which you can literally change your world.

Improving Your Thinking

I'm a professor and a consultant to major global corporations. Whether teaching my students or advising executives, I want to help them improve their thinking by making them aware of how they think and by encouraging them to go beyond their current ways of doing so.

The process is like learning to use a digital camera. First, you have to buy the right one, based on research and your needs. Then you learn the factory's default settings for the camera. These are useful, but often limiting. Lastly, you become imaginative in using the camera's many discretionary options. This requires boldness and a tolerance for mistakes, characteristics of some of the most successful thinkers I've been privileged to know.

Knowing Yourself Better

Recently I saw a banner at a farmer's market proclaiming, "You are what you eat." In other words, what we eat matters—a lot. It occurred to me at that moment that this book is about something even more basic and personal:

You are how and what you think.

If there is one question that the 7.6 billion people on Earth today will all ask in their lifetime (and probably often), it is, Who am I? An exploration of how you think is a step toward answering that question of self-identity.

Your thinking—how you think and what you think about—is your essence. It is who you are. These operations of mind are what make you distinctive. Nothing is more precious and more personal than your mind. That is one reason we are so often reluctant, anxious, and sensitive when putting forward ideas. Your mind is where your "self" lives. If you value that self, you'll want to nourish, exercise, and cultivate your mind and, yes, inspect its workings. All the time! Your wellness depends on it. This book will help you approach your mind with a caregiver's sense of purpose.

* Trademark pending.

Making a Difference in the World

No one's actions are without consequence—even a hermit's life creates ripples that affect other people. If you want to make a positive difference for other people and the world, you need to start by exploring and improving your own mind. That is the best route for improving your life and the lives of others.

A Pact

Those are bold assertions above about improving your thinking, knowing yourself better, achieving greater well-being, and making a difference in the world. They require a special commitment. So I'd like to make a pact, an agreement or contract between me and you. Here's my promise: as a direct result of reading this book and diving into the way you think, you will expand your thoughts and your perspective. You will transform questions into answers. You will have new tools for achieving your goals. You will gain personal satisfaction, and you will be better equipped to make difficult decisions. You will have a better foundation for making a difference in others' lives. And you will have fun in the process.

Now, as a reader, you also have a responsibility in making the above a reality. The journey I am inviting you to take can spark frustration. It can be uncertain. You have to tolerate those states and be willing to take risks and make mistakes. You have to let yourself be vulnerable. It's all part of pushing yourself beyond where and what you are now, of becoming more conscious of your own mind.

So, I ask you to come prepared and willing to experiment in ways that are fun yet sometimes out of your usual comfort zone. Let's promise that we will both do our best to create a meaningful thinking experience that will transform your mind. It's like making a small twist to a kaleidoscope: once you've done it, you can never return to the original pattern.

Why Trust the Author?

You may be asking yourself, Why should I listen to this guy? It's a great question. I've included an addendum at the end of the book that presents some of my career achievements—but I wouldn't want you to mistake those accomplishments for the value they represent.

Let me explain. The value I've gained during the journey of my career comes not from the accomplishments, but from the experiences and learning that came while traveling toward them. The accomplishments are just the milestone markers, reminders that you are on a good path.

My journey and my learning have been and continue to be greatly enriched by the people I meet along the way. Throughout my career, starting as an undergraduate and continuing to today, I have had the good fortune, even the blessing, of being associated with exceptional thinkers. They were and are friends, family, colleagues, and students encountered in the worlds of academia, business, and nonprofit organizations. They didn't walk on water then or now; no one does. But they didn't sink too far, either. They taught me many lessons about thinking and how it affects our own and others' lives. I hope to share these lessons with you.

My Vision for Your Mind's Eye

When thinking about why you, the reader, should read this book I asked myself:

What picture would I like readers to have in their mind's eye as they read the book?

That is, what thoughts and feelings should you experience and what images might I use to reflect them? My vision of an answer appears as the collage above. Don't be startled by it. We'll make sense of it in a moment. Let me just say it is simply my version of a picture you will ultimately form on your own. It represents the experiences I hope you have. Your own collage of images will undoubtedly differ in the particulars, but I'm hoping that the meanings of our collages will overlap nicely.

Now for those meanings.

The large thought balloon represents thinking in action.

The alternating caterpillars and butterflies all around the balloon's perimeter represent the transformational thinking you will encounter: caterpillars are to butterflies what today's thinking is to tomorrow's thinking. Each Think Key exercise in this book contains a caterpillar—an existing way of thinking—from which a butterfly, or new way of thinking, will spring.

Ants, among Earth's most determined creatures, represent the persistence sometimes required to think differently.

The circus scene represents the fun that finding new ways of thinking can be. But like a three-ring circus, the effort can be busy, distracting, and noisy.

The effort can be exhilarating, too—that's represented by the person who has just successfully scaled a mountain. Achieving success is a sweet treat in its own right, indicated by the tasty snack that the climber is enjoying, and it can be financially rewarding too, as shown by the gold bars by his feet.

Of course, becoming aware of one's current thinking and improving it is challenging, like obstacle courses at a military boot camp. It can require hard work, represented by the pickax. These are requisites for successful mountain climbing. When you choose to climb a mountain—or to change your thinking—you also forgo an easier path. That choice is reflected by a fork in the road.

The circus tightrope walker illustrates a willingness to take risks. Taking risks can be scary.

There is good reason to be afraid. Sometimes one fails, like the ice skater in the circus ring. However, this book, like the safety net under the tightrope walker, provides a safe zone for testing and experimenting. Finally, one has to be open to and respectful of the ideas of people who reason differently. Opposing ideas are represented by an elephant and a donkey evenly balanced and face-to-face on a seesaw.

After you finish reading this chapter, I suggest you create a collage like the one above, representing your expectations for this book. What pictures might represent the experiences you are seeking? What do you expect to appear in your mind's eye upon finishing this book? Then compare these images with those that come to mind later and see how your expectations were fulfilled—or changed.

Chapter Two
Unlocking Thinking

The Book's Scientific Grounding

Human behavior is diverse and sometimes bewildering. It is no surprise, then, that there are many ways to study it. Among the disciplines *Unlocked* draws upon are anthropology, demography, economics, history, linguistics, political science, psychology, public health, and sociology, as well as fields that blend different disciplines, including artificial intelligence, behavioral economics, cognitive neuroscience, cultural anthropology, evolutionary psychology, organizational behavior, and social geography.

I don't want to bog you down in a discussion of the various disciplines and their methods, but I do want to stress that all exercises in *Unlocked* are supported by thoughtful research in these fields. The good news is that while researchers often speak in what seems to be a foreign language, their topic is *you*—your thinking and your behavior—and it is quite possible to translate their discussions into simple, practical ideas about thinking.

So, we are not going to be too concerned about the disciplinary origins of an idea. We will be concerned with exploring what these ideas mean for you. A question you might have is, Should we trust the findings from any field of study? The quick answer is yes. The longer answer is, "Yes, but …" Let's clarify this.

The scientific validity of a research finding is ultimately established by diverse researchers testing it using varied methods. This is sometimes called achieving convergent validity. Different people using different approaches arrive at pretty much the same conclusion. This is the primary way of establishing confidence in any idea. While the core idea in an exercise is often highlighted using just one study, and sometimes the original studies are restaged to make them more relevant and accessible, you can trust that the underlying principle is backed by broad multidiscipline, multimethod support.

But your trust should only extend up to a point. Hence, the "but …" added to the second "yes." Because an idea has robust support does not always mean it is correct. The history of human thought and scientific inquiry in all disciplines is partly one of making mistakes and then discovering those mistakes. Making and correcting errors is central to how science progresses. Learning from our mistakes, as good scientists do, leads to better ideas and improved ways of thinking.

Think Keys

Unlocking thinking requires a key. Since you have many ways of thinking, many keys are needed. *Unlocked* provides a bundle of them called Think Keys. Think Key exercises are tools that open doors into your mind's passageways. They help you observe how you think and learn how to be better at it.

I have found it very beneficial when teaching and conducting thinking sessions with executives to create a safe zone, or what Chapter Three discusses as a "thought spot." The atmosphere in a safe zone or thought spot allows people to feel comfortable taking risks. The risks may include looking foolish when advancing a bold thought, contradicting oneself, and making errors. These and other risks are unavoidable when being imaginative.

Each Think Key exercise is a safe zone in which you can freely experiment in the spirit of daydreaming. You can imagine and then try out different ways of thinking without fear of censure. Unless you invite others in, no one is present to observe your use of a Think Key.

Daydreaming, Imagination, and Wondering

Imagining is a daily event. We imagine when we think of the past, the present, and the future. In fact, without imagination we couldn't think at all. You can't—and certainly shouldn't try to—avoid using this important, natural, and powerful tool. It is, however, often undervalued in adult daily life.

Let's reflect briefly on a special instance of imagination: daydreaming. Think back to your childhood: you probably daydreamed a lot. I know I did. (Truth is, I still do.) Daydreaming back then brought me to strange lands and encounters with peril, and it allowed me to ask questions that were never dumb. It often produced wisdom that was precocious and stories about strangers that were invariably fascinating. Through daydreaming, I rehearsed my always-changing future.

This wasn't an attention deficit issue. When as a kid I tossed the winning pitch for the Boston Red Sox in the final game of the World Series or saved a family from a fire or wondered why people don't look alike the way goldfish do, I was deeply focused. It was serious business. It demanded concentration.

On occasion my daydreaming would receive unwelcome attention. In the third grade I was deep into a daydream only to be interrupted by an angry "Jerry! Where are you this time?!" My teacher didn't like being ignored. Having been caught off guard I blurted out, "Canada." The class broke into laugher and for the rest of the day teased me mercilessly about my "trip" to Canada. And another teacher's note about my daydreaming went home to be returned with my parents' signature.

Daydreaming is often demeaned, but it shouldn't be. There is a kind of agility of thought that is acquired by daydreaming. Daydreaming establishes a kind of comfort zone. When we daydream, we are imagining. When we imagine, we are wondering. And when we wonder, we experiment with solutions and actions. The ability to imagine and wonder—to picture what is missing—is a signature feature of our mind.

I am not advocating the willy-nilly drifting of thought that can characterize daydreaming. Instead, I advocate a more fluid yet purposeful daydreaming as you interact with the Think Keys, one that involves identifying your habits of mind, appraising them, and being willing to experiment with new ones. This is a bolder, riskier form of daydreaming. It asks us to dare to be different.

For longer than I care to admit, I failed to connect daydreaming with thinking exercises like the Think Keys. The two ways of thinking seemed unrelated—but in fact, they are connected. Like the Think Keys, daydreaming involves: considerable attention; the making, violating, and otherwise challenging of assumptions; creating stories; mind and body collaborations; a desire to be right; seeing what others don't; problem-solving success; and so on.

Daydreaming fosters a mental agility or nimbleness that I believe distinguishes truly accomplished artists, scientists, scholars, and executives from their colleagues who are simply very good. It is the imaginative *way* they think that makes the difference. And many famous people acknowledge their active daydreaming: George Lucas, the creator of Star Wars, for instance, said, "I spent most of my time in school daydreaming and managed to turn it into a living," and the celebrated poet and novelist Sandra Cisneros confided, "In my youth, daydreaming nurtured me, provided a safe haven."

Summing Up

Earlier I invited you on a journey. Your means of transportation are exercises to enhance awareness of your thinking. Each exercise unlocks the door to a passageway in your thought processes. You may initially react to some exercises with a quizzical "Huh? What's this about?" That is a healthy and not uncommon response. However, it will be quickly followed by "Hmm. That's really interesting! I get it!"

When the exercises are doing their job, you will be more curious about your thinking. The exercises will also free your mind from its habitual routines. Those routines are not necessarily bad, but they can be constraining. And, well, yes, sometimes they can be bad, too.

I chose to call the exercises "Think Keys" because of their power to unlock new ways of thinking, but people have sometimes offered engaging alternative names. Please feel free to replace my term with one you like better. And I'd be delighted if you share it with me.

Just as your thinking has many dimensions, so too there are many more Think Keys than are presented in this book. Every discipline and subdiscipline is chock full of Think Keys. **Unlocked** provides only a sampling, although an important sampling. Hopefully, you will be encouraged to seek out others.

No two people's journey through this book will be the same. You and others will share some elements in how you think, but no two people think identically, even when they agree on many things. You and your friend may share a favorite movie and have similar opinions on what constitutes a healthy snack, but the way you arrived at your shared ideas may be very different—and those different journeys contribute to making you unique.

Further Reading

Stuart Firestein, *Ignorance: How It Drives Science* (Oxford, UK: Oxford University Press, 2012).

Josie Glausiusz, "Living in a Dream World," *Scientific American* 22, no. 1 (March–April 2011).

Mario Livio, *Brilliant Blunders: From Darwin to Einstein: Colossal Mistakes by Great Scientists That Changed Our Understanding of Life and the Universe* (New York: Simon & Schuster, 2013).

Alan Pritchard, *Ways of Learning*, 3rd ed. (New York: Routledge, 2011).

Robert Scott Root-Bernstein, *Discovering: Inventing and Solving Problems at the Frontiers of Scientific Knowledge* (Cambridge, MA: Harvard University Press, 1989).

Dan Rothstein and Luz Santana, *Make Just One Change* (Cambridge, MA: Harvard Education Press, 2011).

Philip Tetlock and Dan Gardner, *Superforecasting: The Art and Science of Prediction* (New York: Crown Publishing, 2015).

Gerald Zaltman, "Marketing's Forthcoming Age of Imagination," *AMS Review* 6 (2016).

Your Notes & Ideas

PART II

Think Keys

Keep in Mind

As we begin our journey a few reminders will help.

1   Most of your thinking occurs before you know it. Nobel Prize winner Daniel Kahneman calls this System 1 thinking. It encompasses the intuitive, unconscious processes that account for nearly all thought. System 2 thinking refers to deliberate, conscious thought.

2   System 1 thinking is not a forbidden-entry zone. Our Think Keys will help unlock System 1 thinking, making it more available for System 2 inspection.

3   The most creative and imaginative people I know make superior use of System 2 thinking to extract brilliance from System 1 content.

Some Guardrails

You are a powerhouse of thought. This is not an exaggeration. A lot is going on in your mind without your realizing it. You are always being curious, sensing problems, evaluating solutions, identifying and selecting options, anticipating their results, and so on. Thoughts are silently swirling away about what to have for dinner, if you should repaint the house, how to explain not turning in a homework assignment, who to vote for, which shoelace to tie first, and the wisdom of changing jobs.

Explaining all this thought-full activity can easily get complicated—unnecessarily so. A couple of guardrails or guidelines will help prevent this.

One guardrail is a principle called Occam's Razor (because it is attributed to the Franciscan friar William of Ockham, or Occam). It states:
With all things being equal, the simplest explanation tends to be the right one.

Another guardrail, also attributed to Occam, is:
The explanation requiring the fewest assumptions is most likely to be correct.

Albert Einstein offers a related guardrail:
Make everything as simple as possible but not simpler.

Making things *too* simple, Einstein suggests, is misleading, like a well-intended but unfortunate fib.

In presenting a Think Key's central idea, I will try to follow the Goldilocks rule, which encompasses these guardrails. You'll recall, Goldilocks wanted her food, chair, and bed to be "just right." Not too much but not too little of what makes those things enjoyable for her. This means keeping explanations as simple as possible short of being misleading. Because readers differ from one another, not everyone will feel I have hit the Goldilocks zone with every Think Key. However, I do hope I come close.

Think Key Organization

Think Keys are presented in small clusters that share a common theme. These are noted below and in the figure at the end of this introductory section. However, these are not the only ways in which Think Keys may be grouped. Most Think Keys in each cluster have close relatives in other clusters. There will be cross-pollination among the Think Keys. To help keep track of this and other stimulation of your mind, a page is provided at the end of each cluster where you can jot notes and ideas that come to mind.

Context

We are always in a setting or *context*. For this reason, I've never liked the phrase "Think out of the box." We are never, ever, not in a box of some sort. Contexts mold our thinking and behavior. Contexts vary, and we may be in more than one context at a time.

Knowledge

Context provides *knowledge*. Once acquired, knowledge has adhesive power. It is hard to "unknow" something. This can be a problem when we have learned different things that conflict. Anyone who has tried to replace a bad habit with a better one knows this.

Memory

Knowledge lives somewhere. It may be in a library, on the Internet, among experts, etc. Importantly, it also lives in our *memory*. An item's life there may be very short, as when we remember the first part of a sentence just long enough to make sense of the last part. But sometimes it is quite enduring, like childhood experiences or our street address. Memory can be very accurate, but also fragile, fallible, and unconsciously altered.

Assumptions

As we gain and retain knowledge, we also acquire *assumptions*.

The two go hand in hand. You'll see how assumptions influence your creativity and problem solving, and how difficult they are to abandon.

Cues

Cues are powerful, often unconscious, signals influencing how we think and act. They prepare us to notice some things and not others. They predispose us to interpret events in one way and not another. Metaphors, physical sensations, color, and word choice can all be cues.

Attention

Cues help direct our *attention*. However, attention is a limited resource. Sometimes we overinvest it in some things and underinvest in others. Rarely is the allocation of attention random. It is influenced by our memories, assumptions, and expectations of the future.

Curiosity

Curiosity helps drive attention. Curiosity helps reduce the discomfort of being uncertain. Thus, curiosity is a vital learning tool. Our survival depends on it. It is the birthplace of imagination.

Explanation

We have a basic need to make sense of things, to account for what is happening to and around us. When we satisfy our curiosity, we have a story to tell, an *explanation* to offer. People are born storytellers. Stories contain connected ideas which are often expressed in terms of causality; if we do one thing, it may cause something else.

Being Right

When developing explanations, we love being correct and hate being wrong. The *drive to be right* or, perhaps, our need not to be wrong, influences what information gains our attention, how we craft our explanations, and our willingness to challenge assumptions.

Metaphors

Metaphors are the representation of one thing in terms of another. They shape our thinking about problems and their solutions, often without our knowing it.

Embodied Cognition

We interact with the world with our bodies as yardsticks. Our sensorimotor experiences are intertwined with our thinking in a process or partnership called *embodied cognition*. The body's role in our minds can be subtle, surprising, and highly influential.

Summing Up

Your pathway through each day requires unconscious and conscious thinking. This thinking involves matters big and small, simple and messy, and from the past, present, and future. We seldom think in a linear way. Your mind is far richer, nimbler, and more complex than that. All of the dynamics (and more) noted in the figure below are operating at once, and a given line of thought may follow any sequence.

The message here? Simple. The Think Keys are fluid. Engaging with them should feel liberating, not intimidating. Have fun with each one. However, do pause to wonder which of the many thoughts in your busy mind a Think Key may help with the most.

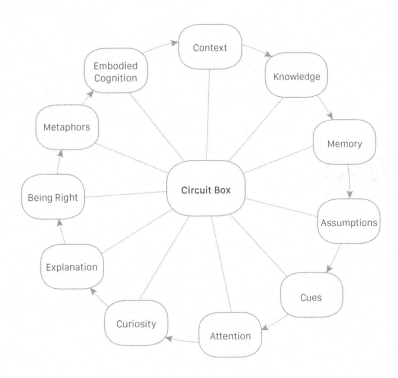

Further Reading

John Bargh, *Before You Know It: The Unconscious Reasons We Do What We Do* (New York: Touchstone Press, 2017).

Antonio Damasio, *The Strange Order of Things: Life, Feeling, and the Making of Cultures* (New York: Pantheon Press, 2018).

Ap Dijksterhuis and Loran F. Nordgren, "A Theory of Unconscious Thought," *Perspectives on Psychological Science* 1, no. 2 (June 2006).

Daniel Kahneman, *Thinking, Fast and Slow* (New York: Farrar, Straus and Giroux, 2011).

Daniel M. Wegner and Kurt Gray, *The Mind Club: Who Thinks, What Feels, and Why It Matters* (New York: Viking Press, 2016).

THINK KEYS:

Context

01 To Disclose or Not

Introduction

Sometimes we have to make a choice where we will be damned if we do and damned if we don't. The consequences are clear, and no matter which decision we make, they are not pretty or nice. This is what makes the choice so difficult. This exercise involves such a decision.

Exercise

Brooke and Jared are sister and brother. Brooke has just turned twelve and Jared is almost fourteen. It is Brooke's birthday, and Jared is taking her to lunch as a treat. Brooke is very excited. Their family seldom can eat out even at fast-food restaurants. Jared has worked very hard to save enough money to take Brooke to lunch, which also requires round-trip bus fares for each of them. It will be a long time before he can save up enough money to do this again.

Brooke absolutely loves burgers. However, she is not an adventuresome eater. In fact, some people say she is a very fussy eater. A new burger joint has opened. It is very popular with her friends, and she hasn't been there yet. The restaurant has quickly become known for its Zomburgers. A Zomburger is made from ground-up caterpillars. It is considered very, very healthy. The burger joint even has its own caterpillar farm to assure freshness and quality. Interestingly, a cooked Zomburger looks and tastes just like a regular burger and is served the same way. After it is

cooked no one can tell the difference. The only thing that sets the Zomburger apart is that it is so very healthy and, of course, what goes into it.

Jared really wants Brooke to join him in having a Zomburger. But after a long discussion at the restaurant in which Brooke often uses the words "disgusting" and "absolutely not!" Jared fails to convince her to try one. She says she'd rather starve. He goes to the counter and orders a regular burger for Brooke and a Zomburger for himself. And French fries for them both.

After picking up the order he heads back to their table. However, while bringing the burgers to their table, Jared realizes he has forgotten which one is the Zomburger. He knows the restaurant people can't help now because the burgers look alike. And he doesn't have any money left to order another regular burger for Brooke.

As Jared arrives at their table, Brooke is looking very pleased and very, very hungry. She can't wait to dig in.

What should Jared do?

1. Give her a burger, pretending it is the regular burger. In other words, keep his confusion about the burgers to himself. He is certain she won't know the difference. How would you justify this decision if you were Jared? How certain are you that this is the best decision?

2. Admit his confusion and let Brooke choose what to do. He knows she feels the Zomburger is disgusting. He will likely end up eating both burgers himself while Brooke goes hungry on her birthday. How would you justify this decision? How certain are you that admitting his confusion right away is the best decision?

3. Should he tell her only while she is eating that he doesn't know which one she has? What emotions do you think Brooke will feel if he does this?

4. What emotions will she feel if he tells her afterwards, say on the way home on the bus?

5. Will her emotional reaction change if he tells her a few years later?

6. How might Jared's feelings be different depending on whether he tells her before she starts eating, halfway through the burger, or right after she finishes?

7. On Brooke's part, should she give a logical reason to Jared for not wanting a Zomburger? Is it enough to say that she finds it disgusting without having to say why? Does she owe him more explanation?

8. If Jared tells Brooke the problem he has before giving her a burger, how do you think Brooke will feel or should feel about Jared?

9. How might the situation differ if Jared and Brooke bought the burgers to eat at home, and Jared only realized his confusion then?

Basic Idea

Situations or contexts that don't appear to have any ethical dimensions to them can, when circumstances change just slightly, suddenly require taking an ethical stance. Often, we are unprepared and have little to no time to reflect on our choices. Instead, we rely on implicit or unconscious ethical standards we barely were aware we had, because occasions to act on those standards rarely arise. The best of intentions, such as providing a birthday treat to a family member or friend, can create a challenge requiring a surprise decision and hence unplanned thinking. Suddenly, a complex ethical issue has arisen. We can be quite sure that Jared, like you as you began reading, was not anticipating the dilemma that arose. The kind of people Brooke and Jared are, the location in which the dilemma occurs, and the consequences of the decisions they will make affect what those decisions will be—and all these factors become highly relevant in the brief moment it takes for Jared to realize his problem.

So What?

Thinking about Jared's situation and how to handle it is one thing, but more broadly, this exercise should prompt you to question how you'll prepare yourself for being in a similar situation. What can you do? When such an occasion does arise, a good question to ask is, What is the foundational principle for me here? That is, what core value do I want to express or use to guide my decision? For Jared it might be, "Never trick anyone to ingest food they don't like." Of course, it could also be, "Don't ruin a very special birthday outing for your sister."

Deciding Whose Life to Save

Introduction

Let's consider a few other difficult and well-studied decision situations requiring immediate action.

Exercise

Situation 1. Imagine a train engineer operating a train. Up ahead the engineer sees five people on the tracks who will be unable to escape the train. The train simply cannot stop in time. All five people will die. However, at the last minute the engineer sees a side track. By acting very quickly the engineer can divert the train onto it. However, there is one person on that track. That person will not be able to escape the train and will die.

Question 1. *What should the engineer do? Divert the train and have one person die or continue ahead and have five people die? Remember, the decision must be made immediately.*

––––

Situation 2. You are standing on a bridge over the train track and see a train hurtling toward five people. This time there is no side track available. But standing next to you is a very large person. If you push that person onto the track in front of the train, it will stop the train before it reaches the five people. Of course, this person will die.

Question 2. *What is your decision? Would you push the big person onto the tracks or not?*

––––

Situation 3. Let's return to the first situation. Assume that somehow you know for sure that the five people straight ahead of the train are escaped convicts. All are absolutely guilty of terrible crimes. The one person on the side track is a young child. You have just enough time to switch the train to the side track if you want.

Question 3. *What are you going to do? Save the five convicts or the one child?*

––––

Other questions to consider:

1. How are the three situations different?

2. Which choice situation is easiest for you? Why?

3. Are your decisions driven only by numbers, or by the kind or type of people the numbers represent?

4. What rule or rules do you appear to be using or would describe your thinking, even if not consciously?

5. For instance, does it matter that you were not responsible for the one person being on the

side track in Situation 1 but would be responsible for pushing someone off the bridge onto the track in Situation 2?

(By the way, most people, about 65 percent in various formal studies, would switch the train to the side track in Situation 1, but only about 35 percent of the people confronted with Situation 2 would push the big person on the track.)

6. When, if ever, would you favor letting five people die while saving one? For instance, if the one person in Situation 1 was a relative or close friend and the five straight ahead were strangers, would your decision be different? What does this reveal about how you value different kinds of people? What automatic assumptions are you making? Are stereotypes you have of different groups or types of people operating automatically in your decision process?

7. Where, when, and from whom did you acquire the values or rules you are using when answering these questions?

Basic Idea

This Think Key starts us off with a reasonably straightforward choice: save five lives or save only one. The number of people who will die is the only distinguishing factor between the two groups. This is what makes the decision fairly automatic. In the second situation, the fact that we must put our hands on the person standing next to us and physically push them to their death to save the other five makes taking that decision harder than taking the equivalent decision in the first situation.

Matters are further complicated in the third situation, when how we value different groups of people comes into play. The life of a child or of a relative may have greater weight for us than do the lives of five convicts. We could substitute other people of different genders, age groups, ethnicities, and so forth and possibly find ourselves face-to-face with our conscious or unconscious biases.

So What?

With the first Think Key, I suggested that a good way to approach an unexpected ethical dilemma is to ask yourself what principles you're using to make your decision. The same is true here. Although the train scenario may seem far-fetched, doctors, EMTs, and members of the police or military do come face-to-face with equivalent types of situation. What principles should guide their—or your, if you are in such a situation—actions? In answering that question, we may have to examine our reactions more closely than is comfortable. For example, if, like many people, you found it easier to direct the train engineer to switch tracks than to push someone onto the tracks to save the five people, why is that? Was it because you take the side of the person standing next to you on the bridge? Was it really *their* side you were taking, or was it your own side because you couldn't bear to be the instrument of someone's death, even to save many lives? You probably didn't think you could be on the side of saving one person at the expense of five others—until you were the one who was forced to put the person in harm's way. These are easy questions to raise, but we don't usually have the luxury of time and discussion opportunities to surface and examine our automatic positions.

Further Reading

Joshua Greene, *Moral Tribes: Emotion, Reason, and the Gap Between Them* (New York: Penguin Books, 2013).

Michael Sandel, *Justice: What's the Right Thing to Do?* (New York: Farrar, Straus and Giroux, 2009).

Context
Think Key | **03** | Social Convention

Introduction

The process of socialization gives birth to countless behaviors in daily life. Socialization refers to the broad ways in which we learn the values, language, and social skills that enable us to live within the norms of a community, whether that community is a family, a classroom, the workplace, or society at large.

We learn both unconsciously and consciously what to do and not do and how to fit in and even prosper. Often, we don't realize how we have been socialized until we encounter very different values, procedures, and skills among people socialized in other communities.

Exercise

In 1990 my wife Ann and I and two academic friends trekked in a very remote area of Nepal. Our goal was to learn how people with no prior experience with photography took photographs. The Eastman Kodak company provided critical support in this effort. In each village, we asked several people to take photographs with cameras we provided. They were given general suggestions, such as that they might take pictures they would want later to remind them of their village if they were ever to move away. If a wedding was taking place, we suggested they might photograph the wedding, etc. However, they were also given quite a bit of freedom in what they photographed.

After several days of doing this in many villages, we had the film developed, and we returned to the villages to give the photographers copies of their pictures to keep. Through an interpreter, we also asked the photographers to relate the story behind a particular picture or set of pictures. This turned out to be a very rich, informative, and surprising experience for the four of us.

For example, we noticed that in many of the photographs people's feet were not visible, while the rest of their bodies were on full display. This puzzled us. We knew that in Nepal (as in many other cultures) it is considered rude to point the bottom of your feet toward other people, but the fact that feet were typically not shown in a photo puzzled us.

Now, a question for you:

1. What is your explanation for why feet were not showing up?

_____

_____

At first, we thought the missing feet were just due to inexperience: perhaps, we reasoned, people were not aware they were cropping the feet out of the photos. During the course of our interviews, however, we soon discovered the real explanation. Not having shoes or other coverings for feet was a sign of poverty. Our photographers did not want to embarrass their fellow villagers by revealing who was poor and who was not. This courtesy could be achieved simply by making sure that no one's feet were captured on film. They were cropped out as a matter of respect, not because the photographers were inexperienced with a camera.

We would never have learned this had we not allowed our Nepali partners to explain their actions from the standpoint of their cultural sensitivities.

Here is another example, involving a different social convention. While in college, I had the opportunity to spend a summer living with a family in Poland. Like most Europeans, they ate their meals with a fork in their left hand and a knife in their right hand. That's where the fork and knife stayed throughout a meal.

Not so for me, not initially anyway. As an American I participated in what they good naturedly called the "dancing utensils."

The dance went something like this:

Step 1. Fork in my left hand and knife in my right hand, cut food.

Step 2. Put the knife down on my plate.

Step 3. Move the folk from my left to my right hand.

Step 4. Place my left hand in my lap.

Step 5. With the fork in my right begin moving food to my mouth.

Step 6. Return the fork to my left hand.

Step 7. Pick up the knife with my right hand and cut more food.

Step 8. Repeat steps 2, 3, 4, and 5 to start eating again.

Step 9. Repeat steps 6 and 7 to cut more food.

You get the picture. And you know who was always last to finish eating despite being very hungry. It was an amusing and unnecessarily complicated dance compared to the family's one- or two-step dining custom.

Of course, in the United States the dancing utensils would never have been noticed. Needless to say, I quickly adopted the local custom during my stay in Poland.

Basic Idea

Social conventions are ubiquitous. Most of you extend your right hand when greeting someone, give up your seat to an elderly person on a crowded bus, likely engage in the dance of the utensils described earlier when eating, and likely hold a door open for others if you are there first and they are right behind you. And yet you might be hard pressed to give a clear reason to a visitor from, say, Mars as to why you do these things. Saying simply that it is the polite thing to do only leads to the question of why that is so—a question you may not have an answer for. And you may not recall when or from whom you learned these things.

Like learning to ride a bike, swim, or blow bubbles with bubble gum, social norms and routines can take a while to grasp, but once learned, they tend to disappear from thought and yet stay with us forever. It takes a foreign culture to bring them to our attention.

So What?

It is tempting to assume that others see things as we do. One message: Don't. And when others see things differently, don't assume they are rude or don't know better—even though sometimes that may be the case. To our Western eyes there were many signs of poverty in Nepal, but the presence or absence of shoes wasn't one we thought to look for. But lack of shoes was a major marker of poverty for our local partners in this project. It is the one they attended to the most.

When I studied visual anthropology and visual sociology, I was struck by the fact that nearly all photos in articles were made by the researchers. The photos captured what the researchers thought were important. They seldom gave their subjects the chance to offer a different perspective. An important question, then, is: How much do you miss by not allowing people with potentially very different viewpoints to challenge yours? Are you allowing people in different social settings or who occupy different positions in a setting you share to challenge how you see things?

Your Notes & Ideas

THINK KEYS:
Knowledge

Knowledge Think Key | 04 | Using Knowledge

Introduction

What we see is partly determined by the external stimuli reaching our retinas. These stimuli create *sensations*. However, our *perception* of those stimuli—what the sensations mean to us—is something we create based on past experience. As other Think Keys show, different past experiences produce different meanings. These meanings form our knowledge. Other sensory systems like taste and touch also operate in this way. Past experience provides the knowledge required to interpret sensory data.

Exercise

Take a look at Figure A below. What do you see?

Figure A   Source: See T. Albright 2012 on next page.

If you are like most people viewing this for the first time, you see a meaningless mixture of black and white splotches. When I first encountered this example, I was reminded of an art lecture I attended long ago. The speaker told a story about an Impressionist painter—I don't remember who—whose untitled painting was confusing to nearly all viewers. They couldn't make out what it portrayed. A local farmer, as the story went, happened by quite coincidentally and noticed the painting. He immediately remarked, "Oh, the waterfall at the edge of my field!" The farmer, unlike the artist's hoped-for patrons, had intimate prior knowledge of the scene.

Now, let's put you in the shoes of the farmer who had learned over the years what this waterfall looks like. Turn the page and look at Figure B there. You should be able to decipher that image with no problem: it's a bearded person.

Now, return to Figure A. What do you see? A bearded person, right? In fact, if you return to Figure A tomorrow, next month, next year, and quite likely beyond that, you will still see a bearded person. You will no longer be capable of seeing only meaningless splotches. Looking at Figure B has provided a learning experience. You have acquired knowledge that will stay with you for a long time.

Basic Idea

While this exercise involves vision, the same lesson applies to our other senses. Our past experiences and our current context make it possible for us to create meaning from the information we take in. Think of it as an active collaboration between the stimuli we encounter and our current and past experiences.

Once we have learned something, that learning helps us make sense of ambiguous but related information we encounter later. In the case of this exercise, memory of what we have learned from Figure B helps us make sense of Figure A when we view it a second time. What was once meaningless now has meaning—meaning that's impossible to ignore. You can no longer see Figure A as random splotches.

So What?

Knowing that present context and past learning affect how we interpret new stimuli, the next time you get into an argument with someone about the meaning of a political, artistic, or advertising message, you can now do something new: you can pause and ask, What is it in our current or past situations and experiences that might account for our differing interpretations? Have you and the person you are arguing with had different "Figure B" experiences that account for your different "Figure A" interpretations? The "facts" of the message you are disputing are less likely to be found in Figure A than they are in your different Figure B experiences. Different prior experiences provided by different contexts can lead to equally legitimate but quite different interpretations of the same current information.

Figure B   Source: See T. Albright 2012 below.

Further Reading

Thomas Albright, "On the Perception of Probable Things: Neural Substrates of Associative Memory Imagery and Perception" *Neuron* 74, no. 2 (April 26, 2012).

When Knowledge Conflicts

Introduction

Sometimes we trip over our knowledge. Different kinds of knowledge, skills, and ways of thinking tangle us up. The result? Confusion.

Note: For readers seeing the following two word sets in this exercise in black and white, please access the Internet and go to https://faculty.washington.edu/chudler/java/ready.html. Follow the instructions provided below for both word sets. The Internet site also provides a timer.

Exercise

For this exercise you'll want to have a timer or stopwatch. Below are two sets of words in different colors. For Set 1, say out loud only the color in which each word is *printed*. Don't say the word that is printed. Use a timer and record how long it takes to say all the colors in the list of words.

Word Set 1

RED	GREEN	BLUE	YELLOW	PINK
ORANGE	BLUE	GREEN	BLUE	WHITE
GREEN	YELLOW	ORANGE	BLUE	WHITE
BROWN	RED	BLUE	YELLOW	GREEN
PINK	YELLOW	GREEN	BLUE	RED

Record your time: _____

For Set 2, do the same thing. Say out loud only the color in which each word is printed. Again, use a timer and record your time.

Word Set 2

RED	GREEN	BLUE	YELLOW	PINK
ORANGE	BLUE	GREEN	BLUE	WHITE
GREEN	YELLOW	ORANGE	BLUE	WHITE
BROWN	RED	BLUE	YELLOW	GREEN
PINK	YELLOW	GREEN	BLUE	RED

Record your time: _____

Basic Idea

You have just completed one of the most well-known tests in psychology, called the Stroop Test.

The time required to complete the exercise for Set 1 should be less than the time for Set 2. Probably a whole lot less. You can repeat this exercise many times and Set 2 will still take longer.

Even though you know your colors well, reading skills are more deeply embedded in your thinking than is color identification. Reading skills are more practiced and operate more automatically.

Skills that operate automatically are said to be implicit or unconscious. Those like color identification that require more attention are said to be explicit or conscious. Thus, implicit thinking occurs without our awareness. Explicit thinking occurs with our awareness. Both types are necessary; neither is in itself bad or good. However, problems can arise when unconscious and conscious thinking come into conflict.

So What?

Our automatic thinking habits can cause trouble when it comes to making judgments. We believe we are thinking carefully even though we aren't— we make assumptions without realizing it, add missing information while believing it was present all along, ignore unexpected information, and use facts to justify decisions made without them. Many Think Keys will explore these and other habits. They will create experiences such as you had when saying the colors in Set 2. They will trip you up, so to speak, and slow you down, and they'll make you aware of hitherto automatic processes—like realizing that when the word "red" is printed in green, you're tempted to say "red," even though you know that you're supposed to say "green."

If you realize you're being affected by unconscious thinking, it's very helpful to press a mental pause button. Stop what you're doing and notice how your different forms of knowledge are tripping you up. In cases where you're making a judgment, ask yourself, Am I aware of what's affecting me? Am I satisfied with how I'm making this judgment? Establishing pause buttons takes some practice, but you'll find the pause required becomes shorter and is used more easily.

Your Notes & Ideas

THINK KEYS:

Memory

Don't Be So Sure

Introduction

I already know your answer to this next question:

Have you ever had an honest argument with someone about who said or did what?
Or who didn't say or do anything?

By "honest," I mean an argument where you and the person with whom you are arguing have truly different memories of an event (versus blaming your bratty sister or office colleague for something you know you were responsible for). You probably don't have to go outside your family to find tons of examples.

Disputes involving memories often include defensive statements like "No, that was *you* who called her a ..." or "No, honest. I have no idea who shaved the dog" or "He hit me first" or "I was nowhere near there when it happened."

Sometimes events or actions are deliberately misreported. But often, things are truly misremembered. We recall something in a way that differs from how it actually happened but believe we are right. We can even "recall" things that never actually happened.

In the next few exercises we'll see how simple words can affect our memories.

Exercise

This exercise has two parts. Think of it as a test of whether you are better at remembering items at the beginning of a list (called a primacy effect) or at the end (called a recency effect).

Part I

Read the list of words below.

noble	castle	crown	king
royal	monarch	throne	servant
jewels	tiara	princess	carriage
court	regal	purple	jester

Done? Now cover the words you just read. Go ahead. It is break time. Have a drink of water or perhaps think for a minute about the last TV program you watched and describe out loud what it was about. Then proceed to Part II.

Part II

Please write down all the words you remember from the list. You can record them in the space below. Don't worry if you don't recall them all. Most people don't. In fact, very few do.

Using the 1, 2, 3 scale below, rate how certain you are that each word you do remember is in the list.

1 = very certain	2 = reasonably certain	3 = not very certain

Words	Certainty Rating
1. _____	___
2. _____	___
3. _____	___
4. _____	___
5. _____	___
6. _____	___
7. _____	___
8. _____	___
9. _____	___
10. _____	___
11. _____	___
12. _____	___
13. _____	___
14. _____	___
15. _____	___
16. _____	___

Finished? You can now check your responses with the original list.

Two questions:

- Did you "remember" any words that were *not* on the original list?
- Did you rate your confidence that they were in fact on the list about the same as those words you correctly remembered?

Your answer to both questions is likely to be yes. That is how the great majority of people respond. Researchers have a lot of experience with exercises like this, and they nearly always see the same results: people remember with high confidence words that weren't present.

For instance, did you also write down "Queen"? The word "Queen" wasn't on the original list. However, about two-thirds of people who participate in this exercise write it down as a remembered word. In fact, you are likely to find that your confidence about words that were not in the original list is about the same as for those that were. You feel equally certain about false and true memories.

Basic Idea

When people recall something incorrectly, they can be quite confident in their memory. In fact, areas of the brain involved in misremembering happen to overlap with those involved in accurate remembering. That may be why our confidence in both types of memory can be the same.

This exercise involved a list of words. I suggested a brief distraction for you, like getting a drink of water or thinking of a TV program. After all, most memories involve something that occurred days, weeks, or years past rather than a minute or two ago. There is ample opportunity for you to add or subtract things from your memory without being aware of doing so.

As we "remember," we create a story. We pull together details that seem to belong to that story, even if in fact they did not play a part in it. The theme in the list for this exercise was royalty. The relatedness of the words in the list made it more likely that we would add in a memory of an obvious example of royalty, like a queen. A queen belongs to the story of royalty. I doubt any of you added the word carpenter or wrestler or pilot. Those simply don't belong to stories of royalty.

So What?

The bundling together of ideas in a memory adds a sense of accuracy, and thus confidence. We have a false—some would call it a misplaced—confidence that we are recalling things correctly when we are not. But the message here isn't that you shouldn't trust your memory. It's just that you should be suspicious enough to double-check it when possible. Be open to the idea that another person's conflicting memory of a shared experience may also be subject to distortion and that you both might be in error.

07 | Priming & Memory

Introduction

Ready for another, similar exercise? Perhaps you could become the researcher for this exercise and have a friend or relative be the subject.

Exercise

Read out loud to your subject(s) the following list of words. As I did with you in the previous Think Key, you might say this is an effort to learn whether they are better at remembering words at the beginning of a list or at the end. After reading the words out loud, tell them a brief story. When you're finished distracting them, ask them to write down the words you read out earlier. Be sure to ask them to indicate how certain they are that each word they write down was in the list you read to them. Use the same scale we used in the previous Think Key:

1 = very certain	2 = reasonably certain	3 = not very certain

Here are the words:

mattress	blanket	pillow	alarm clock
snore	dream	sheet	wake
soft	bedroom	quiet	feather
tired	night	restful	dark

Again, you will find people remembering words not on the list. For instance, nearly everyone "remembers" hearing "sleep" even though it was not read. Nearly everyone gives this word a "1" rating. Some people will strenuously insist they actually heard the word "sleep."

Basic Idea

The last Think Key pointed out that one reason you can have high confidence in elements of a memory even when in fact those elements weren't present is because your mind bundles like things together to improve the overall story—sometimes embellishing that story with elements that weren't actually in it, because they seem to belong.

This Think Key gives you a name for how that happens: priming. Priming occurs when your unconscious mind takes cues, in this case from words like "snore," "dream," and "pillow," and extrapolates from them. What goes with "dream" and "pillow"? "Sleep," of course. Thus, we "remember" that word, even though it didn't actually appear.

So What?

The fact that small, unnoticed cues are all it takes to alter our memories is hugely important when it comes to court testimony or accident reports. Consider people watching the same video of two cars colliding at an intersection. Afterwards, if people are asked to describe what they remember seeing in the *"accident,"* they are unlikely to report seeing broken glass. However, if they are asked to remember what they saw in the *"crash,"* they are likely to report seeing lots of broken glass. This is true whether or not there was any broken glass in the actual video. People remember the same video differently depending on whether they were primed by the word "accident" or "crash." When just the use of a single word as a cue can have such a dramatic effect, you can see how easy it can be to influence—or manipulate— eyewitness reports.

Of course, we do remember many things accurately. But as this and the previous Think Key show, memories are also inventive or imaginative. They add or subtract information and thus mislead us. False memories can be encouraged simply by the words other people use when communicating with us.

08 | Memory & Advertising

Introduction

I'd like to share a childhood memory. It involves a family vacation in New Hampshire. The trip was exciting in part because we were to visit a new place. Even more exciting at the time, we were doing so in a shiny new car, a Packard Clipper. That was something I recall really anticipating. Recently, one of my sisters found photos from that trip. These included pictures of various family members, Lake Winnipesaukee, and the New Hampshire mountains. Some pictures showed one or another of us leaning against the car, standing on the running board, and hanging out the windows. Seeing the pictures was a special treat. I'll return to this memory in a moment.

Exercise

Let's see if we can retrieve some childhood memories of yours, perhaps similar to memories others doing this exercise have had. We'll focus on a possible visit to a Disney theme park.

Imagine you are a passenger in a car listening to the radio. An advertisement for Disney parks begins by broadcasting this headline:

"It's time to remember the magic."

In a soft but energetic voice, the announcer continues:

As we begin to look back at our 100-year history, why don't you take your own look back into childhood ... Try to recall the first time you visited a Disney theme park ... Bring that image to mind ... See Cinderella's castle glisten in the bright sunlight ... Smell the fried foods ... Feel the breeze that cooled off the sweat you worked up as you ran from ride to ride to fit the most excitement into your day. Recall the pride you felt as you cleared the height requirement indicated by the character's wooden hand ... that allowed you to go on the really cool rides like Space Mountain.

You were in your element—festival food, scary rides, and exciting shows. With the song "It's a Small World After All" in your mind, you ventured back to your hotel to rest up for another day. Just then you spotted one of the characters. It was Bugs Bunny! He waved you over. Adrenaline rushed through you, and you somehow managed to move your feet in his direction. He shook your hand. The perfect end to a perfect day.

A voice you imagine belongs to Bugs Bunny adds:

Memories like yours are what make Disney so special ... All of us had the chance to meet our favorite characters up close. It's a memory we share and hold dear as part of our childhood. But the happy memories don't have to end there ... The most memorable, most magical Walt Disney celebration ever is under way now! Come back and see us this summer to relive the excitement!

How would you rate your liking of this ad in terms of the following criteria:

It makes me want to revisit a Disney park:

Agree   1   2   3   4   5   6   7   Disagree

It makes me want to bring my children or friends to a Disney park:

Agree   1   2   3   4   5   6   7   Disagree

It describes my previous visits to a Disney park:

Agree   1   2   3   4   5   6   7   Disagree

It should bring back nice memories for others:

Agree   1   2   3   4   5   6   7   Disagree

Now, please think about the specific experiences you recall from a Disney park. How many of your memories, if any, include Bugs Bunny? Circle below an estimate of specific Bugs Bunny experiences you recall.

0   1–2   3–5   6 or more

Let's return to my childhood memory of the vacation in New Hampshire. The photos, nice as they were, presented one problem:

The car was not a Packard!

Definitely not the car in my memories of that trip. It wasn't even new; it was old and beat up. Yet even today when I think of the trip, the nonexistent Packard still comes to mind first. Until my sister found those photos, I was certain my family had a new Packard Clipper on that vacation. After all, wasn't it a major source of my excitement for the trip, at least as I recalled it as an adult? The car was more prominent in my memory than anything else—central, but misremembered.

Now, what about your memories of Bugs Bunny? You likely reported that Bugs featured at least once in your memories of being at a Disney park. About 50 percent of the people In various studies involving this ad report having a Bugs Bunny memory at a Disney park.

The problem is that Bugs Bunny could never have been at a Disney park. You should have circled "0" above. Moreover, you should not have accepted as true even the possibility of your having encountered Bugs. Bugs is a Warner Brothers character. They compete with Disney and would never allow one of their "properties" or characters to show up in a Disney park.

Basic Idea

Your memory of seeing Bugs Bunny, like my memory of a new Packard car, is false. It is authentic only in the sense of *feeling* true. As we've seen repeatedly in these last few Think Keys, memories are malleable and subject to change over time, even dramatic change.

It is fairly easy to implant false memories. For instance, people who are known never to have been lost in a shopping mall as children have been given a false memory of the experience of being lost. First, they are told that this event took place. When asked to recount the experience, they may initially vaguely recall a mall guard bringing them to their parent. When asked at a later time to describe the experience, they may report that the guard stopped to buy them a treat. And in a still later account, they may describe the treat as having been a particular flavor of ice cream. Essentially, people elaborate over time, creating a vivid recollection of an experience they never had.

So What?

False memories can have a major impact on important decisions. Suppose you are a manager, making a decision about who should receive a promotion at work. Some of the "facts" you base your decisions on may be incorrect—you could be denying or bestowing a promotion in part based on false memories. (Of course, the "facts" being recalled by those affected by your decision may be incorrect as well.)

This doesn't mean we shouldn't rely on our memories when making decisions. We should. Moreover, it is unavoidable. But in important matters, we need to verify those memories if we can. We should not automatically accept our gut feelings—or anyone else's—on a topic. Most researchers say that it is particularly important to seek evidence that memories may be wrong when a different decision would be reached if that were the case.

Further Reading

Kathryn A. Braun, Rhiannon Ellis, and Elizabeth F. Loftus "Make My Memory: How Advertising Can Change Our Memories of the Past," *Psychology & Marketing* 19, no. 1 (January 2002).

Daniel L. Schacter, *The Seven Sins of Memory: How the Mind Forgets and Remembers* (New York: Houghton Mifflin Harcourt, 2002).

Your Notes & Ideas

Assumptions

09 Riddles

Introduction

Life is full of puzzles. You already know that. It is much less full of answers. You already know that, too. And you know that even if an answer seems reasonable, it may not be correct or appropriate. Some of the dynamics involved in choosing the right answer are well illustrated by riddles.

Exercise

Here are a few riddles. Their answers are at the end of this exercise. We'll pay special attention to Riddle 1 after presenting all four riddles, so please don't look at the answers just yet.

Riddle 1:

There is a man at home. Another man is on his way home. The man at home is wearing a mask. What is going on?

Riddle 2:

A man wants to enter an exclusive club, but he doesn't know the password. Another man walks up to the door. The doorman says, "Twelve." The man says, "Six," and is let in. Another man walks up. The doorman says, "Six," and the man says, "Three" and is let in. Thinking he had heard enough, our outsider walks up to the door. The doorman says, "Ten." Our man replies, "Five," but he isn't let in. What should he have said?

Riddle 3:

You see a boat filled with people. You look again, but you don't see a single person on the boat. Why? (Hint: The boat has not sunk.)

Riddle 4:

A boy goes to a booth at a carnival. The carny minding the booth says to the boy, "If I write your exact weight on this piece of paper, then you have to give me fifty dollars. If I cannot, I will pay you fifty dollars." The boy looks around and sees no scale, so he agrees, thinking no matter what the carny writes, he'll just say he weighs more or less. However, in the end the boy ends up paying the man fifty dollars. How did the carny win the bet?

Riddle 1 Revisited

Let's discuss Riddle 1. What do you think is happening here? Write down some of the explanations that occur to you.

1. _____

2. _____

3. _____

Basic Idea

Riddles are engaging. They attract us. Even though we know that they contain a trick, our first response and usually our first several responses are attempts to provide what seems like a straightforward answer to the question. Even if we search for the trick involved, we generally come up with incorrect answers, at least as far as the person posing the riddle is concerned, and different people often provide the same wrong answers. When we learn the "correct" answer, we are genuinely surprised we didn't think of it.

Whether I present Riddle 1 to audiences of managers, graduate students, or my own grandkids, I receive pretty much the same answers. People suggest that a robbery is taking place, a costume or masquerade party is under way, that it was Halloween, or the person at home was spray painting a room or was worried about germs in their home, and so on.

Technically, those are possible answers, but they're not the answers the riddle is aiming for. Only after being told multiple times, "No, that's not it; it is something else" and exhausting all possible answers based on the idea that "home" is a conventional residence do people begin to

suspect "home" could mean something else … like *home plate in a baseball game*. In that scenario, the man at "home" is a catcher, wearing a catcher's mask, and the man on his way home is a batter who has been on base or maybe has just hit a home run.

So What?

Riddles, like jokes, are fun. They hold surprises. They trick us. What is most interesting about riddles is that in trying to solve them, we jump directly to an answer. We do not stop to think about the assumptions we are making that lead us to that answer. Riddles work because their answers are based on assumptions we didn't think about. A riddle's surprise element lies less in the specific answer than in the fact that we never considered the assumption underlying the answer.

An assumption is something we accept without examination. One of my favorite examples involves parents' reactions when their very young child is asked if the world is round. If the child answers yes, the parents are quite proud, because they assume their five-year-old understands a nonintuitive astronomical reality. However, a little probing is likely to reveal that the young child thinks the world is round like a pancake or a Frisbee, not spherical like a tennis ball. The proud parent just assumes the child is picturing a ball.

The problem with assumptions is that like people trying to find the answer to a riddle or parents thinking their child has the wisdom of Copernicus, we may be led astray. It's no big deal if we get the answer to a riddle wrong, and parents can cope with the mild disappointment about their child's spatial awareness, but when problem solving, it's a good idea to examine and question your assumptions. Other—possibly more useful—solutions may then become evident.

Answers to Riddles 2, 3, and 4

To the right are the answers to the other riddles. What assumptions were you making that tripped you up?

Answer to Riddle 2:
Three. He should have said how many letters were in the number he was given.

Answer to Riddle 3:
All the people on the boat are married.

Answer to Riddle 4:
The man did exactly as he would and wrote "your exact weight" on the paper.

10 Invention

Introduction

A distinction is sometimes made between discovery and invention. Discovery involves finding something that has always existed but has never been identified. Invention involves the creation of something that didn't exist before. The two processes can be related, of course. We'll focus here on a discovery but ask you to invent something based on it.

Exercise

You have just read an announcement by NASA about a recently discovered planet. What makes this discovery extra special is that scientists have observed life there. So far, they have only seen one living thing.

Please make a drawing of what you imagine this creature looks like. You can make any assumptions you want about conditions on the new planet and how those might affect the creature's appearance. Please draw your picture in the space below.

Basic Idea

I often used this exercise on the first day of my Customer Behavior Lab class at the Harvard Business School. After people had drawn the creature in their notebooks, I would invite about 20 students to copy their drawings onto the boards at the front of the classroom. Before I tell you what happened next, let me ask some questions and guess at your answers.

1. **At first glance, is your picture weird?**

   You will probably say yes. Usually the pictures range from a squiggly line to very elaborate multieyed creations.

2. **Is the creature symmetrical?**

   You will probably say yes. For instance, even a squiggly line can be cut lengthwise down the middle so that one half pretty much mirrors the other half.

3. **Does your creature have sensory organs like antennae, eyes, ears, tongue(s), nose(s), etc.?**

   Your answer will probably be yes.

4. **Do at least some of these organs come in pairs?**

   Yes?

5. **Are some organs located close together the way your eyes and nose are, or your nose and mouth?**

   Yes again?

6. **Does it have limbs?**

   And again yes?

7. **Do these limbs come in pairs or at least is there an even number of limbs?**

   Another yes?

You can probably guess what happened: the drawings my students made on the board were all similar in the manner suggested by these questions. These questions and their typical answers are based on the properties of animals found here on earth. It is hard to frame a question—or imagine a creature—that is not based on the animals or other forms of life that we know.

So What?

Escaping the confines of what we currently know when imagining something we have never encountered — and may not actually exist — is difficult, perhaps impossible.

- While existing knowledge can be an important springboard for creating new thoughts, it can also be a straightjacket.

- We automatically rely on what we already know when we face a new challenge, whether or not it is appropriate.

- We are often unaware of how very much we are influenced by what is familiar to us.

- It is very easy and natural to represent one thing in terms of another. This is something we'll see in other exercises involving metaphors.

The results of the exercise support these observations. People in my class and elsewhere, when told they can assume any conditions they want for the planet, generally assume earthlike conditions and consequently earthlike creatures.

Further Reading

Mihaly Csikszentmihalyi, *Creativity: The Psychology of Discovery and Invention* (New York: HarperCollins, 2013).

Douglas Hofstadter and Emmanuel Sander, *Surfaces and Essences: Analogy as the Fuel and Fire of Thinking* (New York: Basic Books, 2013).

11 | Assumptions as Architects

Introduction

Before we explore assumptions further, it's worth noting that assumptions are necessary and even unavoidable. They free up thinking space so we can concentrate more fully on matters at hand. Not having to think about everything helps us get through our daily routines and perform important tasks. But because assumptions affect not only our understanding of a problem but also the solutions we generate (as we saw with the baseball game riddle), incorrect assumptions can have long-term, damaging consequences.

Exercise

Assumptions are invisible but active architects designing our thoughts. In this exercise, you will provide examples of those architects at work. You can draw from your personal experiences or use your responses to the other riddles in Think Key 9.

1. Can you think of a time in the past week in which you took an action or made a decision that did not involve making an assumption? It is rare for anyone to make this claim. Even if you didn't make a direct assumption about the action or decision, you almost certainly made assumptions about, for example, the reliability of the sources you consulted before taking the action or decision.

2. Now, how often in the past week have you formally tried to (a) identify your assumptions relating to an action or decision and (b) asked yourself if the assumptions are correct or justified? Again, in case you are wondering, people seldom report doing this.

If they do it, it's usually in response to someone else challenging them.

3. Sometimes we assume something is the case when it is not. Can you provide a personal example or two of times when this has happened to you? For instance, have you ever believed a topic would be covered on a test, worked hard reviewing the topic, only to be surprised when it didn't appear on the test?

4. Contrariwise, we may assume something is not the case when in fact it is. Can you provide a personal example of this type of mistaken assumption?

5. Can you think of assumptions other people have made about you that are or were incorrect? How did you spot these?

6. Why do people—including yourself—find it uncomfortable to have their assumptions revealed and challenged?

Basic Idea

An assumption is something we believe is true or sound enough to act upon. Assumptions are rooted in our unconscious thinking, which is what makes them so powerful and difficult to surface and examine. They present a special paradox: we believe they are true without actually thinking about them.

So What?

Assumptions are strong, hard to detect, and hard to unseat, but because they're limited by our experiences, they can give us "bad intel" when we're in new situations. Wise people will work very hard to free themselves—and others—from the limitations assumptions put on us. I have a good example from a time when I worked as a consultant to a U.S. government agency on issues related to infant nutrition, family planning, and other health topics. The work took place in Latin America. I often worked with the same program manager at this agency. He was based in Washington, DC. A very deliberate decision he made was to provide consultants with as little information as possible until just prior to their departure for an assignment. When asked about this practice he replied:

When I give consultants a lot of advance information, they tend to make assumptions and formulate solutions before they ever arrive on the local scene. These assumptions and the solutions they foster make them blind to the realities of what they will see once they arrive. I've known consultants who draft their final report and recommendations before ever confronting the problem in person. Their initial assumptions prove to be very, very sticky and wrong.

His labeling of assumptions as "sticky" has always stuck with me.

Further Reading
John Bargh, *Before You Know It: The Unconscious Reasons We Do What We Do* (New York: Simon and Schuster, 2017).

12 | Stickiness

Introduction

Assumptions are sticky. They keep reasserting themselves: when they are incorrect, it is as if that is only temporary. We easily slide back into them.

Exercise

Below is an image of two tables. Your first task is to choose the table on which you would prefer to take a nap. (Be assured that there is no risk of falling off the table regardless of which one you choose.) Your second task is to choose the table you'd prefer to have friends gather around to share a pizza.

You probably chose the table on the left for your nap and the table on the right for serving pizza. Nearly everyone—audiences around the globe—makes those same choices.

The table on the left is more inviting to stretch out on, and the table on the right appears to facilitate placement of a square pizza box.

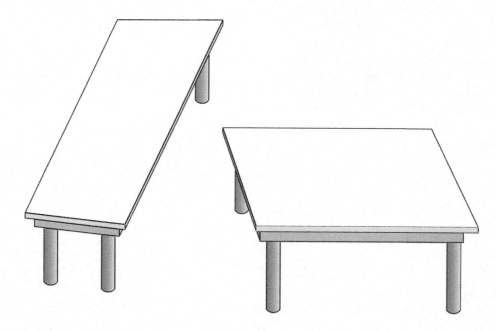

Now measure the long and the short sides of the long table. And measure what appears to be the slightly shorter side and slightly longer side of the squarish table. The short sides of both tables are the same length. The long sides are also the same length. Neither table is longer or narrower than the other!

Now go back to the image and choose again: which table are you going to select for your nap and which one for serving the pizza? Almost everyone chooses the same tables as before for each purpose, even knowing that the two tables are identical. One table continues to *feel* right for a nap and the other continues to *look* most appropriate for holding a pizza container.

Basic Idea

Often, even when we know better, we continue to make choices that are not based in fact or that even are contradicted by facts. We may still experience something as true even when we know it is not. How something "feels" or "seems" often prevails; it continues to shape our judgments and actions even when we know better.

For example, my firm Olson Zaltman Associates conducted a study investigating why people purchased both a famous and expensive name-brand pain reliever as well as the identical product sold for much less money under a drugstore brand name.

The two pain relievers were identical in their ingredients but very different in their prices. Consumers we interviewed bought both, used both, and were confident in their knowledge that both had identical ingredients. So, why were they willing to pay much more for the name brand?

It turns out that people used the name-brand pills when the pain was especially bad, when it was to be given to a family member, or when they wanted to control their pain while they attended an important event. In effect, they discarded their knowledge that the two products are identical in favor of a feeling they might be different. Feelings prevailed over objective knowledge. We will see this again when we discuss magical thinking.

So What?

You may not be able to keep from letting feelings sway your decision making—you may not even always want to. But it's good to be aware of what you are doing. Here are some questions that can help:

1. Feelings power our decisions. How do they differ from what are considered objective facts?

2. In what situations are your judgments most likely to be driven by feelings? By seemingly objective facts?

3. What happens when feelings and facts contradict one another? Are you aware of this when it happens? How much attention do you give it? Which tend to prevail, feelings or facts?

Your Notes & Ideas

THINK KEYS:
Cues

Faces & Instant Messaging

Introduction

Have you ever wondered why human faces look the way they do? Why don't we have faces like wolves or butterflies or fish? Why is our nose close to our mouth and not on a knee? We have two eyes, why not one or three? What do faces do? Why are they important? What information do faces convey? How do people's faces affect our judgments of them?

In this exercise, we focus on the role of faces in our decision making. Specifically, we address how people interpret facial information and what impact that information has on their thinking.

Exercise

Imagine you are about to take a three-hour bus ride. You've made this trip before. Past experience tells you that conversation with the person sitting next to you is likely. These conversations may be brief or last a long while. Sometimes you initiate them and sometimes your seat mate does. This interaction can make the three hours pass quickly or seem to drag on and on.

Seat A   Seat B

As usual, the bus is fully booked. There is no preassigned seating. As you go up the bus steps and turn to go down the aisle, you see that only two seats are available, one on each side of the very first row of seats, just a step away. On one side the vacant seat (let's call it seat A) is next to a person represented by the emoji on the left.

The other vacant seat (let's call it seat B) is next to a person represented by the emoji on the right. (Note: an emoji is used to stress the importance of facial expression and to rule out the added complications of gender, ethnicity, and age-related information that faces convey. These, of course, add to the power of a face to influence our thinking.)

1. Which seat do you choose, A or B?

2. Why that choice and not the other?

3. What influenced your choice?

Most people, if they are in a good mood themselves, choose seat B. When asked to explain why, they usually say something like:

> The person in B looks happy. A happy person is more pleasant to talk with than an unhappy one. The person in A looks unhappy. They are going to be either silent or unpleasant to listen to. That could be a real downer.

This is a choice between experiencing a trip that feels much shorter than three hours or a whole lot longer. And the moods of other people can be contagious. Depending on your choice, you may end up in a better or worse mood when you step off the bus than when you got on.

Now, let's assume you are in a bad mood when you step onto the bus. Are you going to select the seat next to the upbeat and likely chatty person or the person you feel shares your mood and is likely to stay quiet? Experiments have revealed that when people are in a bad mood, they are somewhat more likely to choose seat A than when they are in a good mood.

One more exercise. Imagine you are in the personnel office of a local manufacturing plant. They are hiring people, and you believe you are qualified for the jobs they are filling. You complete your application, have a brief interview, take a couple of tests, and then approach the clerk who helped begin the process. You are instructed to bring your application directly to Mr. Jones, the plant boss. You are told you can find him just outside the door.

As you exit, you notice two men, not just one, standing outside the door. They are wearing identical work uniforms, but you have a clear impression of which one must be Mr. Jones. The two people are depicted below. Which person are you going to approach to introduce yourself and hand your application? Person A or Person B?

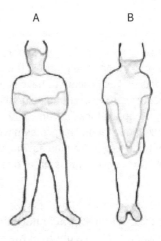

Nearly everyone chooses Person A, whose posture is more authoritative and in charge, as a boss is expected to be. The more submissive posture of Person B gives the impression of an employee who has just been chastised.

Basic Idea

Judgments about the likely emotional tone of future conversations get made very quickly. So quickly, in fact, that in the bus seat example, you take your seat as if you were assigned to it or knew all along you were going to sit there. Basically, you chose your seat (and seat mate) in less time than is required to step into the row. One estimate is that we make judgments based on face appearance in a tenth of the time it takes to blink. We judge a person as a desirable seat mate for a three-hour trip and another as not desirable before we are even aware of the assessment. If someone asks why you chose the way you did before you are fully seated, you might even be at a loss to explain why.

So What?

Evidence suggests that faces have a more important role in human lives than in the lives of any other species. Faces seem to have a single, but complex purpose: to exchange signals with other people. People's faces influence how and what we think about them. The problem with this? We are likely to be wrong. The old saying, "Don't judge a book by its cover," has a great deal of wisdom.

When we find ourselves judging a person as trustworthy or not or intelligent or not using only facial information such as a photo of them or a very quick glance, we need to stop and ask, "What exactly am I basing this judgment on?" The feeling you have, based just on facial features, that someone is trustworthy is far stronger than is merited by more objective evidence. It is not a sound basis for judgment or action. Referring back to the old saying in the previous paragraph, you should go beyond the cover and at least look at the equivalent of the book's table of contents.

As it turns out, body posture is a good table of contents: it's a more reliable indicator of a person's feelings than their facial expression is. The message conveyed by someone's body posture will override the message conveyed by the person's face. For instance, if the happy expression of someone who has just won a sports match is edited onto the body of the loser, the person will be perceived as unhappy. Conversely, if the unhappy expression of the loser is edited onto the body of the winner, viewers will judge the person as happy.

Further Reading

Ulrich R. Orth, T. Bettina Cornwell, Jana Ohloff, and Christiane Naber, "Seeing Faces: The Role of Brand Visual Processing and Social Connection in Brand Liking," *European Journal of Social Psychology* 47, no. 3 (April 2017).

Alexander Todorov, *Face Value: The Irresistible Influence of First Impressions* (Princeton, NJ: Princeton University Press, 2017).

Adam S. Wilkins, *Making Faces: The Evolutionary Origins of the Human Face* (Cambridge, MA: Harvard University Press, 2017).

14 # Reading Faces

Introduction

Let's elaborate on the last Think Key. As mentioned there, we have high confidence in our ability to read faces and sometimes make important decisions using this information, but we're likely to make mistakes when we do so. It turns out reading faces is harder than it seems. The following exercise explores our difficulty in one area: recognizing emotions.

Exercise

There is evidence that facial expression and basic emotions are linked. There is agreement in the academic literature that there are a small number of basic emotions. (Some dissent will be noted shortly.) These include, but are not limited to, joy, sadness, disgust, surprise, fear, and anger. The research literature often explores emotion and faces by presenting faces of people in various emotional states and asking research participants to identify which emotion is being expressed. An example is provided below.

Face A   Face B

Which emotion (joy, sadness, disgust, surprise, fear, or anger) is being expressed by face A? By face B?

You're likely to agree with most people around the world that face A expresses joy and face B expresses disgust. Because so many and varied people agree with your judgment, you probably assume you are correct.

But, giving you a list of emotions to choose from, as is typical in research, provides a prime or cue. It narrows down the possibilities, making the task easier and increasing your confidence in your interpretation.

Here is the catch. Few people spend much time experiencing these basic emotions unmixed with other feelings. Our internal states are much more varied, far richer, and more complex than a listing of a few core emotions. Instead of anger, we may feel frustrated, irritated, unfulfilled, discontented, envious, jealous, and so on. Instead of joy we might feel optimistic, encouraged, hopeful, happy, pleased, relieved, contented, thrilled, enthusiastic, etc. You get the point: our feelings are far more nuanced that a basic emotion label suggests.

Now please look at the photo below.

In a word or two, how would you describe what is going on inside the child in the middle?

_____

Now, if you can, show the photo to others and ask them the same question I just posed to you. Please record their answers.

_____   _____   _____

_____   _____   _____

This is a tough question to answer. It wouldn't be any easier if I asked about one of the other children. Even if you could speak directly with the child, you would still have difficulty answering the question.

Others you've asked about the picture have probably provided a wide variety of responses. An adult class of about 90 people can quickly generate 20 or more contrasting answers.

Basic Idea

We do not hesitate to make judgments about what people are feeling based on their facial expressions, and we are quite confident in those judgments, but it turns out that there are relatively few occasions when we can truly be certain that a given facial expression is expressing a given emotion. Those few occasions may give us a false sense of confidence in our judgments of emotions in much more common or typical situations, where in fact people's facial expressions—and indeed, their emotions—are much more ambiguous. After all, people rarely are in states of undiluted joy, sadness, disgust, etc.

So What?

There is reason to challenge the judgments we make about other people's feelings based on their facial expressions. We are not nearly as good as we believe we are in using facial data. As one authority, Lisa Barrett, puts it when speaking of emotions, "If we put all the scientific evidence together, we cannot claim, with any reasonable certainty, that each emotion has a diagnostic facial expression." A wise strategy then, is to acknowledge your automatic judgment about a face and then try to prove this impression is wrong.

Further Reading

Lisa Barrett, *How Emotions are Made: The Secret Life of the Brain* (New York: Houghton Mifflin Harcourt Publishing Company, 2017). The quotation is taken from page 12.

Priming, Perception, & Action

Introduction

We encountered the concept of priming in Think Key 7, "Priming & Memory." There, a list of sleep-related words primed us to "remember" words that weren't actually on the list. Here, we'll see how word and image cues can prime us to see and do things we might not otherwise.

Exercise

What do you see in the figure below?

Most people see either a rabbit or a duck. About as many people see the duck first as see the rabbit first. After you see the first one, you will eventually see the other one, and then they will alternate back and forth. When people view this image while having their brains scanned with an fMRI, scientists can tell when people are about to see the other animal based on changes in the brain that are visible on the scan, and they can do this before people become aware of seeing the other animal.

Now here is where words come in. If, a few hours before you saw this figure, someone discussed rabbits with you, perhaps in reference to the Easter Bunny or raising rabbits, the chances are very good that the first animal you would see is the rabbit. This would happen even if you did not recall that conversation.

If instead you had a conversation about a delicious roast duck dinner, the chances are very good that the first animal to appear would be the duck—again, even if you didn't think about the conversation.

An anti–drug abuse advertising campaign highlights the problem of images that can be read two different ways. The ads showed lots of drug paraphernalia, which did indeed remind former drug abusers of the hazards this equipment presented—let's call this the duck view. However, the ad also triggered thoughts about the pleasures of using drugs, strongly tempting some viewers to return to their drug use. Let's call that the rabbit view. Once this problem was realized, the advertising was changed dramatically so that only the first thought was likely to come to mind.

Basic Idea

What is especially interesting about the figure of the rabbit-duck is that the same information—the very same drawing—is able to elicit very different interpretations from us. We interpret the "data" in the figure in very different ways depending on what stimuli or words were planted to prime our thinking. This is an important reminder that when two different thoughts are available as ways of interpreting something (a rabbit interpretation or a duck interpretation), one will prevail, but the other may not be very far away.

So What?

It is important to consider whether we are being primed, deliberately or inadvertently, by information presented to us. Then we should determine in which direction the prime is tilting our thinking. It is also important to ask if we are priming others with the words or other cues we use when conveying information. Are our words (or someone else's) emotionally charged? For instance, if we describe someone as "a government welfare recipient," it's likely to bring up a different image from the one conjured if we describe that person as someone "living below the poverty line." (The person described as living the below the poverty line is often seen more favorably than the person described as being on welfare.)

Cues are not limited to words, of course. We can know that two objects are identical except for their color saturation, yet when luggage capacity is important, we'll likely choose the one with a highly saturated color. It just seems or feels bigger. Likewise, a surgical glue whose logo and packaging is changed to give it a more serious look will be much preferred by surgeons over the identical product contained in a more playful-looking package, say one resembling a child's crayon. It is always worth stopping to ask whether an irrelevant cue such as a package design, color, or name is having an undue influence on our thinking.

Further Reading

The Derren Brown advertising agency has a short video that shows just how powerful priming with visual cues can be: https://www.youtube.com/watch?v=YQXe1CokWqQ.

Henrik Hagtvedt and S. Adam Brasel, "Color Saturation Increases Perceived Product Size," *Journal of Consumer Research* 44, no. 2 (August 2017).

16 | Agreement on Words

Introduction

A remark sometimes attributed to Mark Twain is, "The difference between the right word and almost the right word is a really large matter. 'Tis the difference between the lightning bug and the lightning." That difference can have a major impact on how a message is understood. Whether a word is right or only almost right depends partly on who the audience is. The thought a speaker tries to convey with a word or set of words may not be the thought that is understood by the listeners.

Exercise

Which headline below is most likely to catch the attention of both a cannibal and a school nutritionist—A, B, or C?

A. "Scientists confirm the moon is not made of green cheese"

B. "The price of spinach is expected to fall"

C. "Children make healthy snacks"

Most people select headline C. How would you answer the following questions about that headline?

1. What thoughts are cannibals likely to have as they look forward to reading this article?

2. What thoughts are nutritionists likely to have as they look forward to reading this article?

3. If the article is intended for the nutritionists, how is the cannibal likely to feel once they discover this? Angry? Surprised? Disappointed? Curious? Duped? Something else?

4. If it is intended for cannibals, how is the nutritionist likely to feel? Angry? Surprised? Disappointed? Curious? Duped? Something else?

5. How (if at all) do the two audiences' feelings differ? Are they of the same intensity? Is the disappointment the cannibal might experience as strong as the shock the nutritionist might experience?

What examples can you think of where the same words mean different things to different people or even to the same person, depending on the circumstances? Can you think of a harmless and even funny example? How about examples in which different interpretations of the same words could be harmful and serious?

Assume you are the author of the article "Children make healthy snacks," and you are writing for school nutritionists. And let's say you know that cannibals are likely to notice the headline. How would you change it to avoid confusion?

Now imagine the reverse: how would you alter the headline if you were writing for cannibals and did not want to mislead school nutritionists?

Basic Idea

The same words often have different meanings depending on:

- who is expressing them,
- who hears or receives them, and
- the situation in which they are heard.

We saw this in the riddle about the baseball game: the word "home" tends to be interpreted to mean a residence and not home plate.

Consider a couple of other examples. Let's say you see in the business section of your local newspaper the headline, "Fish plant on schedule." You might expect the article to be about a construction project in the town's harborside industrial park. If the same headline appears in the newspaper's sports section, you might conclude the salmon are spawning in the local river at their usual time.

Recently, a relative thanked my wife and me for entertaining him. Now, we know he really likes circus clowns as well as being made to feel welcome. So, shortly after he thanked us we began to wonder: When he said "entertaining," did he mean we were good hosts? I'd like to think so. But he might have meant that he found us goofy and funny, like clowns. We don't really know. Maybe he thought one of us was a clown and the other a nice host and used the same phrase to thank each of us for different things.

So What?

There is an old saying, "It is not what you say, it is what people hear that matters." Of course, what people hear depends on what you say and what they expect you to say. However, it is not automatic for both speaker and listener (or reader) to be on the same wavelength.

Try counting how often in a day or in a specific conversation you hear or say one of the following:

What I mean is … Let me clarify that … I should have said … Let me rephrase that … I'm not following you … Oh, I thought you were saying … You know what I mean … Am I being clear? … What I think you are saying is … Do you really mean … ?

Expressions like these are part of our everyday conversation. They reflect an intuitive understanding that words matter and that we may not be using the right words to convey our thoughts. It is as if we first offer out loud a sketch of our thinking, step back from it, take it in as if we were the audience, and then offer a final, corrected version. We hardly notice the process because it happens so frequently and is so natural.

At the same time, we often fail to self-monitor our statements. We don't wonder whether our chosen word might be understood differently than we intend. This is especially important when using words that may have to be translated into another language. Room for misunderstanding greatly increases in this circumstance. A proposed brand name for a new product tested very well in the United States and was almost adopted by the manufacturer … until the manufacturer discovered it was also a slang term in Spanish for a body part.

Your Notes & Ideas

Attention

17 | Keeping Focused

Introduction

Paying attention is important. This is also called being focused. It seems we are always being told to stay focused when learning something new. When we pay attention, we're better at deciding what information to consider and what to exclude when making decisions. But as the phrase *"paying* attention" suggests, paying attention also requires an expenditure, and we can't spend endlessly. Thus, we have attention budgets. The more attention we spend on one thing, the less we have to spend on something else. As a resource, attention isn't something we can save up for later or borrow from the future for current use. This is why people will joke about not being able to walk and chew gum at the same time. When we try multitasking—for example by trying to drive and text at the same time—the demand on our attention budget can have disastrous consequences.

Exercise

Please do not read beyond this instruction:
open the website below and while watching the
one-minute video, count the number of times
the players dressed in white pass the ball to one
another. Include bounce passes. Be sure to count
carefully.

https://www.youtube.com/watch?v=vJG698U2Mvo

Finished? Good. Continue to the next page.

Two questions for you.

1. How many passes did the players in white make?

2. Now the big question. Did you see the gorilla? (If not, watch the video again.)

Basic Idea

Most people are reasonably accurate when counting the number of passes. They might be off by a couple of passes. After all, the jumble of players is distracting.

It turns out that about half the people who watch this video *do not see* the gorilla. This is true around the world. Of course, once it is pointed out, it is extremely obvious. And yet, on their initial viewing of the video, people who missed the gorilla believed they were seeing everything there was to see in the video.

So just how much of the everyday world around us that we believe we take in do we actually miss?

The answer is, quite a lot. Especially when we've been told to pay attention to something in particular. This applies to everybody. You might think that something unexpected and strange like the gorilla in the video would stand out. However, when our attention has been directed to something else—in this case counting the passes—our mind can ignore even something as startling as a gorilla: it's not important when the task we're paying attention to is counting.

This phenomenon is called "inattentional blindness." We have limited resources for paying attention and have to decide where to spend them. The more attention we give to counting ball passes, the less attention is available to spot a

gorilla. This is a habit of mind we aren't aware of practicing. We really don't have a way of knowing what we are missing—otherwise we wouldn't be missing it.

So What?

All of us are overconfident about how much information we take in. "Surely," we think, "if something is there to notice, I will see it." Wrong. But our false confidence about what we see can lead to overconfidence in the judgments we make. It may contribute to our believing we have all relevant information for making a decision when, in fact, we failed to record important information that was equally available. We need to routinely ask, "What is hiding in plain sight?"

Can you think of situations in your life where inattentional blindness might cause problems? It may be at school, at work, when studying, or when playing a sport, or it may be while driving or walking in the city or country. Are there times when inattentional blindness might help us? What role does it play in our memories? Does it help explain how different people can remember the same event differently?

18 Expectation

Introduction

Let's explore the issue of attention and expectation further. We'll use an example provided by Canon, a manufacturer of photographic equipment.

Exercise

In the YouTube video linked below, six experienced photographers take a picture of the same person. The photographers are not given any direction in how to approach their task, but they are each given a different story about the person they are photographing.

https://www.youtube.com/watch?v=F-TyPfYMDK8

Basic Idea

The lesson here is that how we see something (or someone) is greatly influenced by our expectations, an effect known as expectancy bias. We tend to approach a topic in a way that reinforces our expectations. For instance, if you are told that someone you are to strike up a conversation with at a social gathering is an introvert, you might start the conversation differently than you would if you were told the person was an extrovert. The softer, quieter manner in which you might approach the introvert would likely solicit a softer, quieter response that would only reinforce your initial expectation. On the other hand, the more vigorous, assertive manner you might adopt to appeal to an extrovert might elicit a more extroverted response from the very same person.

So What?

The video ends with the suggestion that a photo is more a reflection of the person behind the camera than of the person or thing in front of it. Like the photographers, different people, given different expectations, will come up with different representations. Expectations shape our processing of information. If we expect to see one kind of person and not another, then that is likely to be the kind of person we will experience. There is a kind of self-fulfilling prophecy. What influences our expectations also influences our judgments.

Our attention budget also comes into play because when a person tells us what to expect, our mind takes that as permission not to spend its own resources investigating further—just as you might not bother working out all the problems on a math quiz if your friend had slipped you the answers. But then again, what if your friend is wrong about those answers? We may not want to spend attention if we don't have to, but sometimes it's worth it.

19 Experience

Introduction

Let's look at how experience affects our attention. This exercise is based on an advertisement for eye-tracking services. Eye tracking is a technology that monitors and records the movement of your eyes as they take in a scene, whether it's a TV advertisement, a billboard, a magazine cover, a favorite family photograph, someone's face or general appearance, a busy street, or pretty much anything else. The technology is quite interesting and readily available.

Exercise

The YouTube video below is an advertisement for a printer. A visual "heat map" of eye movements is presented for three people who have different degrees of experience with photography. Notice how the greater their experience with photography, the more intensely they viewed the scene presented to them, and the more intense the heat map they produced. The heat map shows what is getting the most and least attention, in what order particular details "call to" the viewer, and how long the viewer's eye lingers on them.

https://www.youtube.com/watch?v=lc3suBJDsVw

Basic Idea

Eye movement is driven partly by unconscious thoughts. These, in turn, are planted by or arise from past experience intermingled with current goals and interests. Our eyes move from element to element in a scene as if to answer a question those elements pose. Moreover, the particular sequence in which our eyes move across a scene will influence our interpretation of the scene. That is why artists, including set designers and architects, ask themselves where they want a viewer's eyes to go first, then second, and so on. The order in which people view features and the time they spend with each feature shapes the meaning they derive from what they see.

So What?

Training affects how we look at things: it tells us where it's important to spend our attention budget. Generally, training helps us accomplish a task better. For a photographer, understanding a scene's composition is an important task, so it makes sense that a professional photographer sees more, and more intensely—as represented by the heat maps—than a student or a nonphotographer.

We may be more aware of the biases we pick up with training because they're ones we've consciously striven to adopt, but that doesn't make them any easier to compensate for. It can be very hard, once you're trained in something, to get back to what Zen philosophy refers to as the "beginner's mind." It is difficult to unknow something.

Attention
Think Key | **20** | Silent Distractions

Introduction

Many things compete for and capture our attention. They may even redirect our thinking as we address a problem and make a decision. Even if they don't fully capture our attention, they can be quietly or silently distracting. We saw earlier, for example, how the presence of a verbal cue may bring forward an image of a rabbit instead of a duck when we look at an ambiguous picture.

Distracting events in our environment also have what Lou Carbone of Experience Engineering calls "sticktion," meaning they remain in our minds even when they're not right in front of us—exactly the opposite of the old saying "out of sight, out of mind." They stick with us and affect our decisions and the tasks we perform.

Exercise

How easy is it to rid our minds of a thought? Here is the first exercise.

> Think of a blue polar bear. It can be whatever kind of blue you want.

Take a few seconds to fix this image in your mind's eye.

Have a picture of it in your mind's eye? Good. Here is your instruction. Starting now:

> Do not think of a blue polar bear.

If you are still picturing a blue polar bear (I know you are!) perhaps you could take a short break. Maybe get a snack.

Are you back from your break?

> Are you thinking of you know what?

Of course you are. You have to think of the polar bear in order to try and rid your mind of it.

(If you have a young child or sibling, try asking them, maybe at dinner, not to smile. That is a sure way to produce a smile, not because it is a funny thing to do and worthy of a smile, but because concentrating on the task brings the idea of a smile to the forefront of thinking. The act you are trying to "silence" becomes an active distraction—which is something to smile about.)

Let's go to another exercise. Nearly everyone reading this has a smartphone. On average, people use their smartphone about 85 times a day. That means it is nearby, probably in your pocket or purse, or within sight or easy reach.

A research team wondered if the simple presence of a smartphone affected the amount of attention given to a task and how well the task is done. They had over 500 people perform tasks requiring focus, attention, and novel problem-solving skills. These abilities are common requirements for most school and work settings.

Some people were asked to leave their smartphones in another room. Some were allowed to keep them in their usual place, like a pocket or purse. Another group was asked to place their phones face down on their work desk. In all cases, the phones were put on silent mode.

Imagine you are a participant in that study. Please answer the following questions by circling the appropriate answer:

1. How big a role in your life does a smartphone play? Would you say it plays:
   a. A big role, hard to get along without it
   b. A moderate role, can live without it without much trouble
   c. A small role, don't really use it much

2. Do you think your smartphone sitting in another room and on silent mode would affect your ability to pay full attention to, say, your homework assignment or a report you are preparing for work?
   a. It would make at least some difference
   b. It would make no real difference

3. Do you think your smartphone sitting in your pocket or purse and on silent mode would affect your ability to pay full attention to, say,

your homework assignment or a report you are preparing for work?
   a. It would make at least some difference
   b. It would make no real difference

4. Do you think your smartphone sitting on your desk face down and placed on silent mode would affect your ability to pay full attention to, say, your homework assignment or a report you are preparing for work?
   a. It would make at least some difference
   b. It would make no real difference

These next questions provide an opportunity for you to guess about the research findings.

1. Did most people report consciously thinking about their smartphones while performing their tasks?
   Yes   No

2. What did the research find regarding the influence the location of participants' smartphones had on participants' performance on tests requiring focus, attention, and novel problem-solving skills?
   The smartphone's location mattered a lot
   The smartphone's location mattered somewhat
   The smartphone's location did not matter at all

3. If you answered that the smartphone's location mattered a lot, which location do you think had the smallest effect on participants' performance?
   Another room   Pocket/purse   Desk

4. The greatest effect?
   Another room   Pocket/purse   Desk

Now, the way this exercise is presented probably

tipped you off about the results. Most participants said they did not recall thinking about the smartphone during the exercise. They did, however, greatly underestimate the impact of the smartphone on their task, regardless of where it was located. A smartphone sitting on participants' work desk face down and in silent mode had the largest effect—a negative effect—on participants' attention and ability to solve problems. And this effect was substantial. It seems the mere presence of the smartphone "drained the brain" of attentional capacity, which in turn made it harder to solve problems. The other conditions (smartphone in the other locations) had a similar negative effect, but not as large.

Basic Idea

Proximity of a stimulus (a smartphone, in this case) matters, apparently quite a bit. Out of sight is not out of mind; it is just out of conscious mind. As noted, most people reported not consciously thinking of their phone, regardless of location. Nor did they think their phone's location affected their ability to perform their tasks. But the phone did affect their performance: the more involved they were with their smartphone in general, the greater the negative impact the phone had on their ability to pay attention and perform novel problem-solving tasks.

Stimuli that are objectively absent can still be very present in terms of their influence. Even a smartphone that has been turned off can still

disturb us at an unconscious level. It is as if habit has put us on permanent alert, waiting for it to ring or vibrate, even when we know it is off. This alertness consumes cognitive energy. It uses some of our memory capacity, eats up some of our attention, and introduces distracting "noise" into our problem-solving process.

So What?

Silent distractions operate in the back of our mind, often below awareness. A silent distraction could be a nearby smartphone or some event or idea we are trying not to think about, like the blue polar bear.

Silent distractions take up memory space, divert attention, and interfere with our creative efforts to solve problems. This means we are more likely to rely on unconscious, automatic assumptions, which, as we have seen, can cause problems. Put differently, we are less apt to identify and challenge relevant and automatic assumptions—the ones that are most likely to get us into trouble when making decisions. As a corollary, silent distraction make us less likely to seek and to listen to facts suggesting that we are going down the wrong path and more likely to listen to emotional arguments and those coming from sources of information we like, further cutting down on our ability to critically evaluate information.

Further Reading

Adrian F. Ward, Kristen Duke, Ayelet Gneezy, and Maarten W. Bos, "Brain Drain: The Mere Presence of One's Own Smartphone Reduces Available Cognitive Capacity," *Journal of the Association for Consumer Research* 2, no. 2 (April 2017).

Your Notes & Ideas

Curiosity

Curiosity Think Key | **21** | Uncertainty

Introduction

When hungry, we eat. When tired, we rest. When itchy, we scratch. And when we are uncertain? We become curious. Curiosity is the drive to find out. The need to know is an important, powerful human drive. We all have it. It matters more than intelligence in what we achieve in life. Much of who you are and what you have accomplished reflects how you manage your curiosity.

Exercise

Imagine you have just watched three video clips. Each is about 7 seconds long. In the first, a person is walking on a high wire strung across a river. This person is in full control and nearly finished with the walk. In the second, the person is way off balance. He is about to fall into the river below. In the third, the person is wobbling greatly on the wire, not in full control but not quite about to fall either.

Two questions for you. First, how do you predict each video will end? (Your choices are either A or B, below.) Please also add how certain or confident you are in that outcome as a percentage (100 percent means you are 100 percent sure of your prediction).

    A = The tightrope walker crosses the river successfully.

    B = The tightrope walker falls into the river.

	Prediction (A or B)	Certainty (%)
video 1	_____	_____
video 2	_____	_____
video 3	_____	_____

When students and executives participate in this exercise, most predict success for the tightrope walker in video 1 and express a high level of certainty for this outcome. They're very confident about their prediction for the outcome of video 2, too, only in the opposite direction: they predict the tightrope walker will plunge into the river.

For video 3, about half the people predict success and half predict failure. Most people say they have little confidence in their predictions—around 30 percent or less. People also take longer to decide about video 3.

You are now given a chance to view the ending of just one video. Here is your second question: which video do you choose? Circle one.

video 1: person in full control

video 2: person with no control

video 3: person struggling for control

Most people choose video 3. You probably did too. Its ending is the one with the most uncertainty. It triggers the most curiosity. Let's say you chose video 3 to watch. However, a couple of seconds before it is to be played, you are informed only video 1 is available. How would you feel?

____ Indifferent ____ Angry

____ Disappointed ____ Happy

Most people say they are either disappointed or even angry and want to know why they can't see it. Not only is their curiosity greater after having discussed their answers, they find their continued uncertainty about the outcome irritating. And they now have one more question: why are they being denied the promised viewing?

Some people choose not to look at any of the videos. They report being uncomfortable watching someone in danger. This discomfort overwhelms their curiosity about the ending. You, too, have likely felt that way at times. So, another question:

Can you think of occasions when your discomfort has overwhelmed your curiosity? (Hint: What about the time you covered your eyes or fought the urge to do so while watching a frightening scene in a horror movie?)

Speaking of questions: about how many questions is a child around the ages of three or four likely to ask in an hour when with a caregiver? The answer is below.

Basic Idea

From birth, we are curious. Without curiosity, infants would never grasp much about the world around them. As language skills develop, spoken questions become curiosity's voice. Young children may ask as many as a hundred when, how, why, and where questions in the span of an hour. Whether the question is trivial or not, the asking requires significant sophistication: an awareness of something you don't know, a desire to know, a belief an answer exists, and a feeling someone else might have it.

It is said that the human mind is a prediction-making machine, fueled by curiosity about which of our predictions are best. This is not an idle, fun-to-know kind of curiosity. Survival and general well-being depend on it. This is one reason why everyone—you included—is born curious.

So What?

The capacity for curiosity can be enhanced or diminished. Helping others enhance it is one of the greatest gifts we can give. It is a nice gift to give ourselves, too. You are doing this, of course, with *Unlocked*.

How can you further nurture your curiosity? Two vital ingredients, in addition to those discussed elsewhere in *Unlocked*, are open-mindedness and self-criticism. These two qualities not only enhance curiosity, they help satisfy it. They are at the heart of curiosity's dual nature: the drive to know and the satisfaction we get from finding out. Here are some guidelines:

- Favor restlessness over contentment; be on the alert for improvements to be made.

- Look for irregularities or outlying information that may be a harbinger of things to come or that may represent unexploited opportunities; avoid the temptation to dismiss them as flukes.

- When you reach a conclusion, ask how it might serve as a beginning for a new and better idea or action.

- Have the courage of your convictions, not someone else's, as you explore unfamiliar and perhaps unpopular territory.

- Avoid the automatic tendency to dismiss opposing judgments or information suggesting you might be in error.

Further Reading

Jakob Hohwy, *The Predictive Mind* (Oxford, UK: Oxford University Press, 2014).
Ian Leslie, *Curious: The Desire to Know and Why Your Future Depends on It* (New York: Basic Books, 2014).
Philip Tetlock and Dan Gardner, *Superforecasting: The Art and Science of Prediction* (New York: Crown Books, 2015).

22 | Hedgehogs & Foxes

Introduction

A Greek parable tells of the difference between a hedgehog and a fox. The hedgehog knows one thing well. It is curious about that one thing but not about much else. It tends to be overconfident in the narrow zone of what it knows. The fox has a limited knowledge of many things. However, its curiosity doesn't go deeply into any of them. The fox is a "jack of all trades, master of none." It jumps from idea to idea with enthusiasm but without staying power, soon moving on to something else.

Exercise

Let's think of the hedgehog's knowledge as being flashlightlike. That is, it has a long, narrow beam. The fox's knowledge is more like the light from a weak lantern. It sheds light widely, but not brightly. My questions for this exercise are:

When have you been the victim of hedgehog behavior and not had the curiosity to look outside the narrow beam of the flashlight's cone of knowledge?

When have you been the victim of fox behavior and not had the curiosity to go deeper into a shallow if broad cone of knowledge?

When have you created a fox-hedgehog partnership, in effect using a flashlight and lantern together?

To clarify the last question, let me illustrate. Someone who wants to build a house is foxlike. He or she must know many things about home construction—about electrical work, plumbing, finished carpentry, and so on. However, this person does not specialize in any of those things. To have them done, he or she will call in an electrician, a plumber, etc. Those tradespeople are the hedgehogs. Together, the fox and hedgehogs form a solid team. Their complementary skills come together and get the job done.

What examples from medicine, manufacturing, education, government, and elsewhere can you think of in which hedgehogs and foxes team up? Consider this: not all team members are human. When has information technology been your flashlight? Your lantern?

Basic Idea

You might have been expecting me to ask if your curiosity is more like the hedgehog/flashlight or the fox/lantern. I'm not going to do that. I don't like pigeonholing people and don't believe you should do it to yourself. There are undoubtedly areas of your life in which your curiosity is shallow and areas in which it is deep, areas in which it is broad and areas in which it is focused.

Generalized and specialized knowledge are both important, but alone, both are insufficient. This does not mean a new breed is called for, no "feges" or "hoxes" or "flanterns" or other such things. Those would be just additional pigeonholes to avoid. Rather, what's needed is the ability to recognize when a particular way of knowing is needed and how to collaborate with someone who knows things in that way.

So What?

I recommend always asking yourself both "Am I thinking broadly enough?" (i.e., is my mental peripheral vision wide enough?) and "Am I being focused enough?" (i.e., do I need to drill down further?) To put it another way, you can invoke a switching rule that says, "I need to become more foxlike/less hedgehoglike" (or vice versa). Or seek out complementary skills. You might ask, "Do I need to bring in a fox or a hedgehog to help me solve this problem?" The important task is to recognize when the problem would benefit from a broader scope and when a more focused scope is called for and to be open to integrating that into your perspective. We should always ask, "What lies outside the long, narrow beam of my flashlight of knowledge?" and "What lies outside the broad but weak scope of my lantern of knowledge?"

Beyond the Obvious

Introduction

This exercise builds upon the previous one. A metaphor can reveal and hide information at the same time. (This will be discussed in more depth in later exercises.) We may be so caught up by a metaphor's imagery that we don't look past its surface message—to draw on Think Key 22's foxes and hedgehogs, we interpret a metaphor with a hedgehog's narrow focus.

Exercise

A friend and colleague, Professor Luc Wathieu of Georgetown University's McDonough School of Business, asks his business students this question:

"What makes a great pirate?"

Recently I posed this same question to a number of businesspeople and added a second question:

"What can we learn from the qualities of a great pirate?"

Please list your answers to both questions. A photo of Johnny Depp as Capt. Jack Sparrow is provided to stimulate your thinking.

Great qualities:

_____

_____

_____

What can be learned:

_____

_____

_____

Now, let's switch gears for a moment. Consider two more exercises. What do you see in the picture below? An elderly woman, right? A bit peculiar looking perhaps but still an elderly woman. What else do you see? Quite likely nothing. Now turn this page upside down. What do you see now? Yes, a young woman.

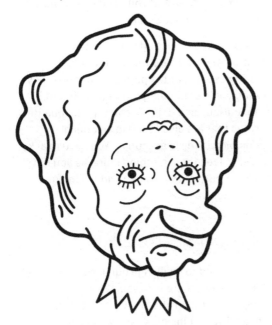

By changing the orientation of the image, what you see changes dramatically.

One more. What do you see in the next image? If you are focused on the black area, you will likely see a vase. If you focus on the outside white space, you will likely see two faces. It all depends on what you look at. You don't see both at once. Studies in neuroscience assure us of this fact.

Now, let's return to the pirate questions and compare your answers with those the businesspeople provided. There are no wrong or right answers, of course. Some respondents noted the Robin Hood-like nobility of "robbing from the rich and giving to the poor," while others described a "vigilant opportunist" who "steals wherever, whenever, and from whomever" he can. Other people mentioned an abundance of weaponry, a ruthless crew, being a gifted liar, compulsive greed, a secret treasure map, a sixth sense when navigating, knowing who and when to bribe and threaten, living for today, decisiveness, and the like. Do your responses resemble these?

Many people suggested that there was nothing to be learned from pirates, even great ones. Who, they asked, would want a pirate as a role model in their home, their school, or in their workplace? Some wondered what I was driving at with the second question. Does that puzzle you, too?

Other people, though not as many as I expected, responded differently. They stopped thinking about the fact that the qualities belong to a pirate and started looking at the qualities themselves. They realized that some of the very qualities that can make someone successful at piracy might also make a person a great—and ethical—leader in other domains. Put another way, the qualities that make a person bad at other jobs (laziness, shortsightedness) make a person bad at piracy, too. Among the positive qualities they mentioned were ability to focus on the job at hand, knowing when to delegate tasks, building loyalty in the organization, being imaginative and engaging in unconventional thinking, understanding value, being a sound planner, having a map, taking risks, being alert to unexpected opportunity, and so on.

The people who couldn't find anything to be learned from the pirate's qualities employed a mind-set equivalent to looking at either of the two pictures above and only seeing one image. The people who could see value in the qualities of a pirate had an instinct to change their orientation—to turn the question upside down and see how some qualities that make a person a successful pirate are relevant to managers who are not pirates at all. This is like asking what might surround the black space of the vase. Did this occur to you?

Now, you might wonder why I didn't just ask directly about the qualities of a great business or government leader. I have done that in the past, and I know Professor Wathieu has as well. However, when we have asked the question that way, what we have received by way of replies are popular but often empty buzzwords.

Basic Idea

Some things to be discovered are right in front of us. Seeing them, however, requires a different way of looking. When a business professor asks students or business colleagues about the qualities of a great pirate, you should suspect the pirate is a metaphor, and you need to ask what it reveals and what it may hide.

The negative facts relating to piracy and the reputation of pirates are the distracting, obscuring aspects of the pirate metaphor—they can keep you from finding the value in it. But if you are curious and dig, you can find the qualities of pirates that are also found in an ethical, responsible business executive. You have to ask yourself to look for something more, as you did with the picture of the woman and the image of the two faces/vase.

So What?

We always need to challenge our assumption that we have seen all there is to see. We should have our eyes open for an alternative view that might produce different insights. Are we missing something that's right in front of us? It is surprising how infrequently this question arises. When someone else sees what we miss, we often say, "Why didn't I see that?!" That question occurs too often. A few fundamental questions to ask, implicit in many of our Think Keys, are: Am I being curious enough? What am I missing as a cue? What change in perspective do I need? What am I most uncertain about? What disconfirming evidence about a position I have taken am I missing or even avoiding?

24 Reflections by Notables

Introduction

Famous people are generally known for their bold thinking, imagination, creativity, and actions. They are known for daring to be different and for their hard work and persistence, often under discouraging conditions. We often remember particular statements they make that encapsulate important ideas about thinking. Interestingly, although any individual statement is the expression of a particular person, the ideas expressed are often commonly held by many famous imaginative thinkers. That is, I believe most people quoted in this exercise would agree with most of the statements made by the others.

Exercise

A sampling of wise insights is presented below. Select two examples that appeal to you—or, If you prefer, by all means use a quote found elsewhere.

⸺

Every great advance in science has issued from a new audacity of imagination.

— John Dewey (1859–1952), philosopher

Fortunately, somewhere between chance and mystery lies imagination, the only thing that protects our freedom, despite the fact that people keep trying to reduce it or kill it off altogether.

— Luis Buñuel (1900–1983) film director

To invent, you need a good imagination and a pile of junk.

— Thomas Edison (1847–1931), inventor

The mere formulation of a problem is far more often essential than its solution, which may be merely a matter of mathematical or experimental skill. To raise new questions, new possibilities, to regard old problems from a new angle requires creative imagination and marks real advances in science.

— Albert Einstein (1879–1955), physicist

Logic will get you from A to B. Imagination will take you everywhere.

— Albert Einstein

Every child is an artist; the problem is how to remain an artist when you grow up.

— Pablo Picasso (1881–1973), artist

If you hear a voice within you say, "You cannot paint," then by all means paint, and that voice will be silenced.

— Vincent Van Gogh (1853–1890), artist

Never limit yourself because of others' limited imagination; never limit others because of your own limited imagination.

— Mae Jemison (b. 1956), astronaut

I like to think of ideas as potential energy. They're really wonderful, but nothing will happen until we risk putting them into action.

— Mae Jemison

You can't wait for inspiration, you have to go after it with a club.

— Jack London (1876–1916), novelist

Imagination is the beginning of creation. You imagine what you desire, you will what you imagine, and at last, you create what you will.

— George Bernard Shaw (1856–1950), playwright

Creativity comes from a conflict of ideas.

— Donatella Versace (b. 1955), fashion designer

Curiosity about life in all of its aspect, I think, is still the secret of great creative people.

— Leo Burnett (1891–1971), ad executive

Creativity is just connecting things. When you ask creative people how they did something, they feel a little guilty because they didn't really do it, they just saw something. It seemed obvious to them after a while.

— Steve Jobs (1955–2011), entrepreneur

Imagination is the Discovering Faculty, pre-eminently. It is that which penetrates into the unseen worlds around us, the worlds of Science.

— Ada Lovelace (1815–1852), mathematician

Research is formalized curiosity. It is poking and prying with a purpose.

— Zora Neal Hurston (1891–1960), novelist

If you shut the door to all errors, truth will be shut out.

— Rabindranath Tagore (1861–1941), writer

There's a part of me that's always charging ahead. I'm the curious kid, always going to the edge.

— Yo-Yo Ma (b. 1955), cellist

_____

Which two people or quotes have you selected?
_____ and _____

1. Why do your selections appeal to you? What makes each statement wise? _____
   _____
   _____

2. What would you like to ask the people quoted about their thoughts? _____
   _____
   _____

3. Review the list of quotes. If you could change one—including one of your two chosen quotes—to make it even more meaningful to you, what change would you make? _____
   _____
   _____

4. When might the wisdom offered in the quotes you chose backfire on you? _____
   _____
   _____

5. When and why is the wisdom offered in the two quotes you chose difficult to act on? _____
   _____
   _____

When teaching, I sometimes distribute fortune cookies on the last day of class. These contain various messages or ideas expressed during the course. For instance, "Nothing is more subjective than a number" or "Not everyone who wanders is lost" or "Have the courage of your convictions" and so on. So, here is another question.

6. As a teacher or a parent, what special quote would you give to your students or children to inspire or encourage them to dare to be different in their thinking and actions? That is, what quote would you put in their fortune cookies? Please don't feel you need to limit yourself to the quotes provided above— feel free to find another quote or make up your own statement. _____

   _____

   _____

7. Why is this special quote important to you?

   _____

   _____

   _____

Basic Idea

Selecting quotes may have been difficult, perhaps because several appealed to you. They all hold a special meaning even if you have trouble explaining why. We might as well try to explain why chocolate ice cream tastes so much better than strawberry ice cream (or vice versa). It just does. And you don't need to explain why in order to enjoy it.

Still, there is value in understanding why we resonate more with one saying than another. For example, do we tend to avoid conflicting ideas and thereby miss the creative opportunity such conflict provides?

(See Versace on previous page.) Do we need to invite more conflict and critique of our ideas in order to stimulate curiosity? Does the appeal of Van Gogh's quote reflect our awareness of an overly active inner critic that needs to be silenced?

So What?

Other people's thoughts on how minds operate are an important source of learning. Other people may be friends, family, coworkers, or famous people we've never met or others we've never heard of before. The important point is that when a statement about thinking differently and more boldly resonates with us, we should try to understand why.

Recall that in the third question, I asked if there was a way you could modify one of the quotes I offered to make it even more appropriate. For example, the Jack London quote ("You can't wait for inspiration, you have to go after it with a club") came up among a group of executives in a large global company headquartered in London. They were complaining about the lack of time to develop and pursue new ideas. Not having time to think, they argued, was killing their inspiration and creativity. They began brainstorming about "clubs" to wield to get the necessary time. It became apparent in the process that they needed to amend the quote to make it more relevant to their particular division. The amended quote became "Inspiration is success, you have to go after it with a club."

Your Notes & Ideas

Explanation

Introduction

People are born storytellers, not only of "Once upon a time ..." tales but other types of stories as well. Stories are our mind's inventions based on the discovery of a few items of information. Sometimes very few items of information. The information we lack is often provided by our assumptions and other cues operating below awareness.

Exercise

I've used the picture below with audiences around the world. Nearly everyone responds the same way. Let's see if you do, too.

Source: Roger N. Shepard

Two questions for you:

1. Which monster is bigger?

2. What is happening in the scene?

Please answer these questions before proceeding.

———

Most people quickly say that the monster on top is bigger. Usually, with a little hesitation, they also say something like: "The big monster has an angry look and is chasing the small monster in the hallway. The small monster has a frightened look and is running away."

Is this pretty much what first occurred to you?

Now, measure the size of the two monsters. Go ahead. Or, look at the image at the end of this Think Key. The monsters are the exact same size. Now, look closely at their faces. They are also identical.

Basic Idea

Assuming you reacted to the picture as described above, how did you conclude that the monster on top was bigger? Probably you didn't even think about it. You just knew. Why? How did you automatically arrive at this judgment?

It is likely that your brain, with the help of your eyes, records both creatures as being the same size. However, you also perceive a long hallway. And your unconscious mind is busy at work without your knowing it. Your unconscious mind has learned something about objects in the distance in hallways. Based on this learning, your mind appears to reason as follows:

Since both monsters are in a hallway and the one at the top is further back, it must be bigger, maybe a lot bigger. After all, if the monster in front were moved further back, it would appear smaller because things look smaller the further away they are. Since the monster further back doesn't look smaller, it must be a lot bigger than the one up front.

This is an illusion, of course. Placing the monsters in the hallway creates a 3-D experience for us. It fools our unconscious mind into experiencing the two monsters as being of different sizes.

As for the expressions on the two monsters' faces, we conclude the "bigger" one is angry since it appears to be chasing the "smaller" one. Our unconscious mind concludes that anyone being chased by a big monster with an angry look ought to be scared. So, we also "see" a frightened look on the "smaller" monster's face.

The hallway encourages us to make these assumptions. We don't have to think about it; in fact, it happens without our conscious thought. We automatically feel or know this is what is going on. Interestingly, it turns out that people who live in settings where hallways are uncommon just see two identical monsters.

So What?

We all carry different kinds of "hallways" in our minds. They are a source of our assumptions. It doesn't take much to bring forth assumptions. I remember an incident while grocery shopping with my mother when I was a child. A little kid (not me!) brought a bag of candy to his mother for her to put in the cart. His mother just blew up. She shouted at the top of her voice, "Put it back now! Do it!"

I thought, "What a mean mother!" But I also recall my mother saying, "That poor mother. I'll bet that kid has been nothing but trouble for her all day long." My mother and I had very different assumptions about what the day had been like for those two people. We were seeing that mother and child in two very different hallways, and that influenced our interpretation of the candy-bag-in-the shopping-cart blowup. Our different assumptions and past experiences automatically produced two very different stories about the scene. I absolutely knew the kid was generally well behaved but had a really mean mother. She was the pursuing monster in the hallway. My mother was equally convinced the kid had been pure trouble all day. For her, he was the pursuing monster.

The question we all need to ask is, What hallways
are we carrying around that shape the way we
weave a story with the information at hand?
Hallways are littered with assumptions, and we are
always in a hallway.

Having looked at the image to the right, return to
the first one. Does one monster still look bigger
than the other? It's likely that you still experience
the one on top as bigger despite knowing they are
the same size.

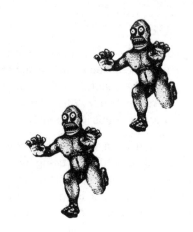

Further Reading

Donald D. Hoffman, *Visual Intelligence: How We Create What We See* (New York: W.W. Norton & Company, 1998).

Roger N. Shepard, *Mind Sights: Original Visual Illusions, Ambiguities, and Other Anomalies, With a Commentary on the Play of Mind in Perception and Art* (New York: Macmillan Learning, 1990).

Explanation Think Key | **26** | Anomalies

Introduction

Consider the story "The house that Jack built," which introduces children to a cow with a crumpled horn that tossed a dog, that worried a cat, that ate a rat, and so on. Whenever I heard this story as a child, I was full of questions like "Who crumpled the cow's horn? Why? How did they do it? How would I do it? Does the cow know? Does it hurt? Why just one horn?" For me, the crumpled horn was easily the most interesting element of the story.

To get at the same point from a different angle, think about the difference between the expression "taking a life" and "killing someone." As we saw earlier, words matter. "Killing" and "taking a life" have the same consequence for the victim; the act is the same. Yet the word "kill" is more blunt and direct. If I asked you to describe both a life taker and a killer, I bet your description of the first would be more generous. Which phrase makes you more curious about the person being described? Which description would prompt you to read more if you could only read about one?

Exercise

The photo to the right shows two empty water containers. The one on the right is unblemished. The one on the left is all dented and banged up. Your job is to choose one to write a short story about. (No, you don't have to write a story, though I'd be very curious to read it if you do.)

Photo by Gerald Zaltman

Which container have you chosen for your short story? The one on the left? The one on the right? Nearly everyone chooses the container on the left. When I do this in a class or similar setting, I often have the two containers within everyone's sight long before I get around to them. Later, people comment their eyes were constantly being drawn to the rumpled container.

Like the word "killer," the rumpled container invites our curiosity. It has a mysterious past! It contains irregularities that invite explanation and storytelling. It catches our eye by raising questions we'd like to have answered. What happened to it? Who did it? Why? How does it feel now? I was recently swimming at a YMCA. A number of young children in the pool were happily and noisily ignoring their adult supervisor. At one point, however, they became strangely silent. I looked up to see a man with one leg commencing to enter the pool. He had every child's rapt attention. I have little doubt he triggered their questions and storytelling.

Basic Idea

Anomalies attract us. Deviations from the routine or the expected engage us. Faces with slight irregularities are judged more favorably and looked at longer than those with perfect symmetry. True, we can miss an anomaly such as a gorilla moving through a group of people passing a basketball—but only when we're asked to spend our attention budget elsewhere.

So What?

It is said that fortune favors the prepared mind. The mind that nurtures its attraction for anomalies and searches them out—the mind that is prepared to tell stories about those anomalies—is a mind that can benefit from accidents or serendipity, the source of many important discoveries, including penicillin and X-rays. The challenge is to deliberately seek irregularities in what we see or in the information we collect. We have to guard against trying to prove points and seeking only confirming evidence. We need to be on the alert for irregularities that can help us improve ideas or even discover new ones—it is not enough to wait until they jump out at us. This requires explicitly asking about irregularities that are present in our information. The early detection of anomalies can lead to the identification of new trends in the marketplace, new product opportunities, and the emergence of potential problems.

Reasoning Forward & Backward

Introduction

In general, we don't like uncertainty and coincidence. We try hard to explain things that puzzle or confuse us. Human history, for instance, abounds with varied explanations for natural phenomena such as the Northern Lights, eclipses, volcanic eruptions, and the changing of the seasons. Many of these explanations later proved to be scientifically incorrect, and that history of error is reason for us to be humble about many of today's explanations, scientific or not.

Exercise

Let's start with Situation 1. Later, I will ask you to imagine having a clone of yourself who responds to a second situation without knowledge of the first situation—though that will be a challenge since what you think at one point in time influences what you think later.

Situation 1

You are given the following information:

John is a tightrope walker for a circus.

He doesn't use a safety net.

If he falls, he will end up on crutches.

Then you are told:

Today John is using crutches.

1. What do you think is most likely to have happened to John? _____

   _____

2. Using a scale of 0 percent to 100 percent, how confident are you of your answer? _____ percent

3. What else might have happened to him?

   _____

Situation 2

Now it is your clone's turn. Your clone is unaware of your answers to Situation 1.

Your clone is given the following information:

Today John is on crutches.

Then, only after learning this, your clone is told:

John is a tightrope walker for a circus.

He doesn't use a safety net.

If he falls, he will end up on crutches.

1. What is most likely to have happened to John?

_____

2. Using a scale of 0 percent to 100 percent, how confident are you of your answer in Situation 2? _____ percent

3. What else could have happened to John?

_____

Basic Idea

Situation 1 starts with a possible cause. It first establishes John as having a dangerous job. This is followed by a possible effect arising from this job: falling and ending up on crutches. Situation 2 starts with an effect, being on crutches, and ends with a description of a possible cause, being a tightrope walker.

When questions like those posed in Situation 1 and 2 are given to equivalent groups (like you and your clone) two things happen. First, people responding to Situation 1 typically express much *higher* confidence in their guess about what happened than do people responding to Situation 2, and people responding to Situation 1 tend more often to guess that John fell off the tightrope.

Second, people responding to Situation 1 often generate many fewer explanations about what might have happened to John than people responding to

Situation 2. Remember, the same information is provided in both cases. And usually, in the end, the same cause is favored: John fell off the tightrope.

As noted, the first situation starts with a *cause* whereas the second starts with an *effect*. The different responses reveal an important tendency:

We have a natural bias to prefer thinking *forward* from an apparent *cause* to an effect, as in Situation 1. We are not quite as comfortable thinking *backwards* from an *effect* to a cause, as in Situation 2.

In Situation 1, people are presented with a possible cause that can account for the effect that they're later told about. Having been given an obvious and plausible cause, they stick with it with confidence; they are not inclined to generate alternative causes. In Situation 2, people are given the effect first and immediately start trying to guess at a cause, even before learning the information about the tightrope. They generate more alternative explanations and thus have more options to choose from, and their confidence level—in whatever theory they go with—tends to be lower.

So What?

The fact that we find it easier to reason from a cause to an effect than the reverse explains why so much advertising employs forward reasoning ("Our brand [a cause] produces better results [effects]") rather than "If you want these results [effects], use our brand [a cause]." A forward-thinking presentation leaves less room for consumers to think of other brands that could provide the same benefits.

Explanation Think Key | **28** | Why versus How

Introduction

People are constantly seeking explanations for things: Who did this? Why did they do it? How did they do it? When did they do it? And so on. Such questions reflect an inborn curiosity and also fuel further curiosity. Asking who did something naturally leads to wondering why they did it and to our attribution of causes of their actions if they are not around to tell. We are all natural historians in this way. Attributing causes to effects is fundamental to learning and essential to survival. Two common questions are why did something happen and how did it happen. Interestingly, it is sometimes difficult to distinguish between the two.

Exercise

Imagine yourself as a four-year-old. You are in the kitchen with your parents. The tea kettle on the stove has just started whistling as the water reaches its boiling point. You ask a simple question:

Why is the kettle whistling?

One parent responds:

"Because the electric coils on the stove became hot and transferred their heat to the kettle. That makes the water molecules get very busy and produce steam. The steam tries to escape, which makes a whistling noise as it goes through the narrow opening of the kettle."

Your other parent responds more simply:

"Because I want a cup of tea."

A few thoughts for you:

1. Which response best answers the question for you as four-year-old? Was it the "how does it happen" question the first parent answered? Or the "what purpose is being served" question the second parent answered? Most people imagine a four-year-old having in mind the question the second parent answered.

2. Of course, maybe you had neither question in mind. You just wanted attention and had learned that asking questions caused your parents to give you attention.

3. Which answer would have satisfied four-year-old you most? You probably would have been happier with the second parent's answer. It is short. It is simple. At four, you understand human wants much better than you do fluid mechanics.

4. Which parent, the father or the mother, were you picturing as giving the answer involving fluid mechanics? And which parent were you picturing as giving the answer involving their desire for tea? Traditional gender roles put "science-y" things in the male realm, so perhaps you pictured the father giving the first answer. Having decided that the first answer is the father's, that leaves the second answer belonging to the mother.

Basic Idea

Both parents' answers are acceptable responses to the question. Satisfying the need for a hot cup of tea requires activating the dynamics of fluid mechanics, among other things. But the two answers also involve different causes. One draws upon science and the other on human wants. The two causes aren't mutually exclusive; the two parents simply understood the nature of the question differently. That might be due to the kind of question they preferred to answer. We have biases for certain types of explanations, and this can influence both the way we frame our own questions and, as in this case, the way we interpret other people's questions.

So What?

It is easy to be trapped by a familiar and obvious causal explanation. However, when we rely on a familiar way of explaining things, we miss out on the opportunity to discover or acknowledge other possible causes of the same event. (We'll visit this issue again when discussing the law of the instrument.) This may lead to settling for incomplete and shallow explanations or, worse,

incorrect explanations. This happens when we don't bother to probe the inner layers of the onion, so to speak, to find out what lies behind the causal factor we have identified.

I was invited to join a discussion among managers of a national hardware chain. The issue being addressed was why people spend less time in their hardware stores than in local supermarkets. The managers had settled on one particular cause: evidence that people typically have many fewer items to buy when visiting a hardware store than they do when visiting a supermarket. The managers noted that they also seldom observed people in hardware stores with shopping lists, whereas people frequently bring shopping lists into supermarkets. It's certainly true that the number of items to be purchased directly influences the time spent in many retail stores. However, this causal explanation was not true *enough* to solve the problem of how to increase store traffic, time in store, and purchase levels. Management had failed to ask what was it about their store operations that caused customers to buy less and spend less time browsing.

By failing to ask if there were other less obvious but maybe more impactful causes of the negative effect they were trying to address, the managers had missed a basic factor: store design. A store's layout affects customer comfort levels and inclines or disinclines them to browsing. I brought the managers' attention to evolutionary psychology. This field tells us that early humans were uncomfortable in crowded, chaotic, jungle-like settings. They were more comfortable in open settings like savannahs. Crowded, chaotic settings such as jungles obscured both dangers and food, whereas in more-open settings such as savannahs, early humans were better able to spot both. Evidence suggests that those long-ago learnings persist with us in modern life. The company's hardware stores, it turns out, created uncomfortable jungle-like settings. Customers wanted to get out as quickly as possible. This desire to escape was not operating, or at least not to the same degree, in supermarkets. Adding more products, including some of the goods found in supermarkets, to the hardware store's offerings was unlikely to induce people to spend more time in the stores.

Management made a number of changes to their stores' layout based on what they learned from evolutionary psychology. The subsequent increase in the average number of items purchased per customer visit was directly attributed to those changes.

29 | Magical Thinking

Introduction

You may be familiar with the "rally cap." This is a baseball cap turned inside out and worn backwards. It is believed to help your team rally from behind during critical moments in a close ball game. Fans and players in other sports have similar practices. These superstitious practices are examples of what's often called "magical thinking."

Exercise

Magical thinking is making a causal connection between actions and events when there is no supporting scientific evidence for the connection. For instance, a very successful baseball player, Wade Boggs, ate chicken before every game because it helped his batting average, or so he believed.
A young colleague of mine wears the same pair of socks every time he gives a speech. He claims the speeches are more successful when he wears them. Some people believe getting out of the wrong side of the bed will make them grumpy all day. (Of course, if there is a wall on the wrong side and you jump out on that side, you'd have good reason to be grumpy.)

> Can you make a list of your own magical thoughts?
>
> What about magical thoughts among people you know well?
>
> What are the benefits of magical thinking for you?
>
> What is your evidence?
>
> Any downsides?
>
> Any evidence of those?

Note: In my experience, almost everyone is able to think of at least some magical thinking of their own, even if not right away. Interestingly, people who at first have trouble identifying examples of magical thinking tend to agree with the following statement:

> It is bad luck to be superstitious.

This, of course, is magical thinking! And in spite of believing that statement, these people will say that they support the magical beliefs of others. For instance, they too will wear a rally cap at a baseball game in support of their friends.

Basic Idea

There are many situations where we believe one thing causes another while also knowing there is no rational explanation for the connection. The rally cap is one example, but here is another: A family I know is very dedicated to their local sports teams. When their football team plays, family members wear special clothing, sit in the same family room locations, have the same foods, etc. These household "rules" have evolved over time. Rule violations are taken seriously. (I am quite sure I have never been forgiven for violating the seating rule by not sitting in the "guest chair." At halftime, with the team hopelessly behind, I was "invited" to change seats. It helped somewhat as the game went into overtime, but their team still lost. I was the unspoken cause.)

Their magical thinking appears to work. Most of the time their team wins. When their team loses, I'm told it is because of unique forces like bad officiating, the absence of a star player, or violation of a household rule. (On rare occasions a loss is simply accepted with a philosophical "You can't expect to win every single game.")

Magical thinking reflects just how strongly motivated we are to find and assign a cause to some event we can't explain rationally. We don't like surprises, have a hard time accepting coincidences as merely coincidences, and want very much to be in control. So, we invent causes, especially ones we can control, and connect them to effects. We employ good-luck charms and rituals in an attempt to assure success or favorable outcomes. Once we form a belief about the connection between events, like wearing our ball caps inside out and backward to help our team rally from behind, we are very reluctant to give it up. The belief has staying power even in the face of contradictory evidence.

So What?

We tend to dismiss people, especially from the past and from different cultures, as credulous and foolishly superstitious, but fail to see that we can also hold illogical beliefs, subscribe to superstition, and urge other to do so as well. We believe bringing an umbrella on a walk will stave off rain, whereas forgetting one will bring a downpour. Being superstitious relieves our uncertainty. When we discover someone has brought a banana onto the fishing boat, we now have a good explanation for why the fish aren't biting. It gives us a false sense of control. The banana gets tossed overboard and it is, "Fish on!"

Sometimes, magical thinking may discourage productive, careful thought. Good-luck charms and rituals displace logic and reason and provide false feelings of constructive behavior. Whenever we engage in magical thinking, we need to ask, "Really? Would I bet on this? What purpose is my magical thinking really serving?"

Your Notes & Ideas

Being Right

30 | Right versus Wrong

Introduction

One of the most basic distinctions we make is between right and wrong. We make this distinction everywhere. We do it in matters of ethics, in multiple-choice answers on tests, in social situations like choosing friends or a list of people to invite to a party, in business decisions, while shopping, and when voting. Sometimes the benefits of being right are trivial and sometimes huge. And likewise, the cost or penalty for being wrong can be insignificant or very big. Because questions of right and wrong are pervasive and the consequences of a decision can be substantial, we take the matter of right and wrong very seriously.

Exercise

Which statement most describes you? Circle only one, A or B, even if both apply.

A. I love being right.

B. I hate being wrong.

Done? Let's explore this further.

Basic Idea

This is an exercise I often present to executives during interviews. They often hesitate and wrestle with which option to choose, perhaps much like you just did. But, when pushed, they usually choose option B. This is the option most people—but not everyone—choose regardless of the context.

It seems there are many more opportunities for being wrong than for being right. We all know this is true in school. Often the penalties for being wrong are greater than the benefits of being right. At work, you might get a raise if you are right a lot, and that is nice. But you might get fired if you are wrong a lot, and that most certainly is not nice. We are told that the first thing doctors are taught is to do no harm. That is, avoid being wrong.

It can be more unpleasant looking silly (or thinking we do!) in front of classmates when we are wrong than it is pleasant when we give the teacher the right answer. This is especially true when asking a question. People are often afraid to ask questions for fear of looking bad. Paradoxically, questions are the basis for all learning. (Of course, fear of looking bad may have some basis if the question has an obvious answer you missed by not doing the reading assignment, or if it was answered earlier while you were daydreaming. We've all had experiences like these.)

So What?

There are two consequences of being right or being wrong that affect us. Every day. First, the fear of being wrong reduces our willingness to be imaginative. It can reduce our chances of success when we do try to be imaginative.

It is as if people think, "If I am *too* imaginative, I am more likely to be wrong, so perhaps I'll hold back and avoid trouble or embarrassment." Of course, this also reduces your chances of a big success and the joy that comes with it.

Second, wanting to be right causes us to seek out facts and evidence that justify our ideas or actions and are helpful in convincing others we are right. This makes it more likely they will cooperate with us. We certainly don't want them thinking we are wrong. As a result, we look for reasons that support our ideas and ignore those that don't. Unfortunately, evidence suggesting we are wrong can sometimes be used to make our ideas better. It's like ignoring the fact that you used too much brown sugar in making candied bacon—you miss the chance to learn how to make it better next time.

To help address these consequences, I always encourage my students, clients, and colleagues to do *premortems*. A postmortem, of course, is something that occurs after someone dies or after a business or government decision has been declared a failure. The postmortem tries to figure out what went wrong. In a premortem, you stop and ask:

> Okay, what if this decision or choice turns out badly? What is the most likely explanation we'd find?

Basically, in a premortem, you ask what *could* go wrong as opposed to what *did* go wrong. Then you determine if you know enough about the situation to be pretty sure that what could go wrong won't happen. If you don't know enough, you need to investigate further.

31 Law of the Instrument

Introduction

Our minds tend to obey rules, one of which is known as "the law of the instrument." This law says:

> If you give someone a hammer, pretty soon the whole world begins to look like a nail.

When we are experienced with and skilled in using a tool, we see it as relevant wherever we look. Early in my career, I was very interested in a field called "the diffusion of innovations." This field studies the success and failure of innovative ideas, practices, and products. It classifies people as innovators, early adopters, early majority, late majority, and laggards. It also characterizes various stages of something catching on in society and has special ways of viewing innovations themselves. I applied the classifications and stages from this field to nearly everything. Collectively, those classifications were my favorite hammer. I tended to ignore the fact that sometimes it took effort to squeeze things into this framework and that other theories and viewpoints might be more appropriate.

A tool or instrument can take many forms. It may be:

- A professional perspective, such as thinking as an anthropologist, a psychiatrist, or a law enforcement officer
- A favorite theory of behavior, as in my example above
- A research tool, like a survey or focus group
- An action, like voting on strict party lines, even when unfamiliar with the candidates
- Magical thinking, like always wearing something blue on important occasions
- Habit, like always taking out-of-town guests to the same restaurant
- An outlook, like being optimistic.

No one is immune to this law. Consider medical-student syndrome. This refers to medical students believing they have the illness they are currently studying. That illness becomes a hammer for assessing health symptoms they are personally experiencing at that time. Another example involves research methodologies in various sciences. Sociologists often use large surveys to study issues. Psychologists often use formal laboratory experiments for the same issues. Each group formulates the problems they study in ways that bend to or favor the primary research method they learned as students. Consequently, each group develops different insights about the same issue.

Exercise

Let's explore the law of the instrument to see how current beliefs act as a hammer shaping how you think about the future.

Please answer the questions in Sets 1 and 2. Space for your answers is provided after Set 2.

Set 1

    a. Do you prefer Coca-Cola or Pepsi?

    b. Do you prefer Android or Apple mobile operating systems?

    c. Are you a Democrat, Republican, or Independent?

Now, answer Set 2 questions.

Set 2

    d. In 20 years, will more people prefer Coca-Cola over Pepsi, or will more prefer Pepsi over Coca-Cola?

    e. In five years, will Android be more widely used than Apple, or will Apple be more widely used than Android?

    f. In 20 years, will a larger or smaller proportion of Americans be [insert your party preference]?

Be sure to write your answers to questions a, b, and c under Set 1 below. Then write your answers to questions d, e, and f under Set 2 below.

	Set 1 Current Personal View	Set 2 Beliefs about the Future
1. Coca-Cola/Pepsi		
2. Android/Apple		
3. Political affiliation		

Basic Idea

Let's stay with your answers in this exercise. Did you tend to answer Set 2 questions in the same way you answered Set 1 questions? A study of nine different topics, including the three you just addressed, found between 64 percent and 91 percent of the respondents felt the future (Set 2) would show an increase in support of their current position (Set 1).

Put differently, regardless of how popular or unpopular people saw their current position, they felt that in the future more people would support their current position than do now. A current view becomes a hammer used to estimate what is likely to happen in the future.

All of us (yes, including you) have several preferred tools we use over and over—some we use at school, some we use at home, some we use at work, and so on. These tools may be stereotypes we have of certain people or cultures, or preferred solutions to problems. We are typically unaware of our preferred tools' operation.

Offsetting the downsides of the law of instrument requires understanding (a) your personal biases for and against particular points of view, (b) the nature of a problem to be solved, and (c) the ideal contours of an appropriate solution. A deliberate brainstorming of alternative "hammers" is also helpful. One constructive way to approach this is to ask how someone from another country, discipline, socioeconomic status, etc. might see and approach the problem. What can you learn from their perspectives?

So What?

The law of the instrument applies broadly in all areas of life, and its operation is unavoidable. That, in itself, is not a bad thing. The problem comes when we fail to anticipate its operation and hence don't notice what instrument we are using, which means we can't ask whether our chosen instrument is appropriate.

Further Reading
Todd Rogers, Don A. Moore, and Michael I. Norton, "The Belief in a Favorable Future," *Psychological Science* 28, no. 9 (September 2017).

| **32** | # Clairvoyants & Wizards

Introduction

Let's say you have a superpower. However, I am going to limit your choice of what it can be. This may be challenging in the way you were challenged to choose between being right or not being wrong. Both options may be attractive, and in reality, our choices are not necessarily between just one or the other.

Exercise

Two people are waiting at a bus stop. They recognize each other as frequent riders on the same bus, so they start up a conversation and share information about themselves.

One person turns out to be a *clairvoyant*, someone who can see the future. Maybe not in precise detail, but enough to see how most things happening now will develop in the future. This person is not 100 percent accurate, but pretty close.

The other person is a *wizard* who has the power to fix problems. The wizard can't fix every conceivable problem, but can fix most problems that arise from decisions or events that have downsides. They have a general conversation about what it is like to have their talents.

A few questions.

1. If you could be just one of these people, who would it be, the clairvoyant or wizard? Why? What appeals to you about the abilities of the character you chose? What doesn't appeal to you?

2. What turns you off about the character you didn't choose? What does appeal to you?

3. Would you rather not be either one? Why not?

4. Why do superheroes often have dual identities? (Think Superman and Clark Kent).

5. If you could ask the clairvoyant just one question, what would you ask? Does this question affect anyone besides you? Why this question and not another? Is this a case where something popped into your mind without much inner debate or thoughts about alternative questions?

6. If you could present just one problem to the wizard to solve, what problem would it be? Is this more of a personal problem, or is it a social problem affecting many people? Why this question and not another? How hard was it to select a problem?

7. How might life be difficult for the clairvoyant? For the wizard? Do you think they are happy having their superpowers? Do you think they publicize them? Hide them? Don't care if anyone knows?

8. If you were a clairvoyant or a wizard, how would you decide which questions—or whose questions—to answer or problems to solve? Would you shield someone from an answer they might not want to hear? What if the solutions to a problem did not work in favor of the person asking? Would you still solve the problem? What if the solution had a bad consequence for someone else?

Basic Idea

Having a special competence in anticipating the future does not, of course, necessarily exclude having special competence in fixing problems. However, each is sufficiently uncommon as a highly developed skill set that the two talents are not likely to be found in the same person. At the same time, it can be said that everyone does have some of each. And both talents have special moral responsibilities and require different types of knowledge.

So What?

A favorite research topic for me is how people approach messy or ill-structured problems. These are problems for which there is no clear solution or at least no good solution. Often it isn't even clear what the problem is, just that there is one. I or my colleagues often interview executives at length on this topic, and I always had students in my consumer behavior class go through a two-hour metaphor elicitation interview on the topic. The interview is a special way of uncovering what people feel they know and what they feel they don't know, or are unaware of feeling. It stresses an analysis of the metaphors they use to express their thoughts and feelings.

Many interesting patterns surface in these interviews. Like you, everyone can see the benefit of both clairvoyance and wizardry when a problem is messy or unclear. Nearly everyone expresses concern with seeing the future. And nearly everyone expresses concern about formulating solutions. However, there is also a tendency for interviewees to favor one power or skill over the other. Moreover, not surprisingly, people seem to gravitate to the skill that comes most easily and naturally. For instance, some people are especially adept as seeing what others would call the unexpected consequences that might unfold because of a possible action. Other people are more adept at formulating solutions that involve the least compromise among stakeholders.

The challenge is to ensure that a decision team has both types of people—both the clairvoyants *and* the wizards. If you are facing a messy problem on your own, role-playing both the clairvoyant and wizard roles will help you address it more successfully.

Your Notes & Ideas

Metaphors

33

Metaphors Shape Thought

Introduction

We often describe one thing as being like something else. For example a sports reporter might write, "Trying to tackle [a football team's star running back] is like trying to catch a greased pig." *Greased pig* is a metaphor for the hard-to-tackle running back. It has been estimated that English speakers use about six metaphors for every minute of speech, or 10 or more for every 25 words we speak. (Sports, incidentally, is rich in metaphors: it is estimated that there are about 1,700 sports metaphors in common use.)

Although we often use metaphors deliberately, we just as often use them without realizing it. Metaphors' ability to slide into our minds and conversation without our awareness make them especially powerful—not to mention sneaky. In this Think Key, we'll talk about a kind of metaphor known as a simile: an explicit comparison between two things.

Exercise

Imagine a friend is describing John, who is someone you don't know:

"John is as clumsy as an ox."

Your friend then describes Elizabeth, also someone you don't know:

"Elizabeth is as clumsy as a cat."

On a scale of 1 to 10, where 1 = graceful and 10 = clumsy, how clumsy do you picture John being? How about Elizabeth?

You likely have little doubt that John is quite clumsy, whereas Elizabeth is quite graceful. "Ox" and "cat" are similes your friend uses to describe how John and Elizabeth move. You may not ever have seen an ox, but the expressions "big ox" and "clumsy ox" are used so often in English that if John is described as clumsy as an ox, you have an impression of him as a big, lumbering creature. Cats you most likely have seen, but even if you hadn't, expressions like "cats always land on their feet" will have given you the impression that a catlike person is sure-footed and graceful.

For that reason the word "clumsy" feels strange in the second sentence.

Now, let me ask another question. How intelligent do you think John is?

Very Intelligent   Very Unintelligent
1   2   3   4   5   6   7   8   9   10

Using the same scale, how intelligent do you think Elizabeth is?

Very Intelligent   Very Unintelligent
1   2   3   4   5   6   7   8   9   10

And another question. Among males of John's age, how strong do you think John is?

Very Strong   Very Weak
1   2   3   4   5   6   7   8   9   10

What about Elizabeth when compared to other females of her age?

Very Strong   Very Weak
1   2   3   4   5   6   7   8   9   10

Oxen are also associated with strength and with stupidity ("dumb ox," "strong as an ox"), whereas cats are considered clever (even to the extent of having nine lives attributed to them), so when people are asked to rank John and Elizabeth's intelligence, they tend give John low ratings and Elizabeth high ones. On strength, John is rated stronger than other males his age. Cats aren't associated with either strength or weakness, so Elizabeth is considered to be about the same as other females her age. All those judgments arise from comparing John to an ox and Elizabeth to a cat.

How else might you describe John and Elizabeth as clumsy and graceful, respectively, using similes? What extra meanings might these other similes convey? For instance, what added image would you have of John if he were described as being as clumsy as a drunken moose or as clumsy as a toddler? How about if Elizabeth were compared to a ballerina—or a shark?

Basic Idea

The famous biologist Edward O. Wilson tells us:

> Without the invention of language we would have remained animals. Without metaphors we would still be savages.

Metaphors are a basic way of thinking, not just a way of packaging and delivering an idea, and they are powerful. Even with similes— explicit comparisons—we're influenced by characteristics other than the one being used in the comparison. Your friend used similes to describe how clumsy John and Elizabeth were, but the other associations of "ox" and "cat" affect your perceptions of John and Elizabeth too, as the intelligence and strength ratings show. John may not actually be strong—but thanks to the comparison with an ox, you imagine him to be.

So What?

Everyone uses metaphors, whether or not they are aware of it. The use of metaphor boosts our imagination, and imaginative thinking is rich thinking. One proof? Metaphor is strongly associated with major discoveries and inventions.

It is important to be aware of our own use of metaphor when attempting to understand how and what other people think. As this Think Key shows, a single word ("ox," or "cat") can create strong, complex associations. Very deliberate attention is given to this in the development of advertising and political messaging. We always need to ask what idea a metaphor is trying to convey and what other ideas may be riding along. The next Think Key continues this exploration.

Further Reading

Denis Donoghue, *Metaphor* (Cambridge, MA: Harvard University Press, 2014).

Edward O. Wilson, *The Origins of Creativity* (New York: W.W. Norton & Company, 2017), 161.

Gerald Zaltman and Lindsay Zaltman, *Marketing Metaphoria* (Boston, MA: Harvard Business School Press, 2008).

34 Body Metaphors

Introduction

Our senses can shape and convey abstract ideas that do not involve the senses directly. We may say, for instance, that a particular song stinks or that there is something fishy going on, though no actual odor is involved. However, our senses do more than just help in expressing thoughts. They also influence how we develop thought—just as the characteristics we associate with oxen and cats affected our thoughts about John and Elizabeth in Think Key 33.

Exercise

This exercise asks you to try to have a conversation with someone for more than a few minutes without using metaphors that involve the senses or other physical references. You might try this in your next phone conversation, dinner conversation, or even text messaging. After you have done this, please return to this exercise.

How often did you find yourself using metaphors involving your body? Not sure? That is not surprising. These metaphors are so automatic we aren't aware of using them. However, as we'll see, it is hard to carry on a conversation without leaning on body-based metaphors. Think of these everyday examples:

Don't let your enthusiasm *run away* with you.

He has a *nose* for investments.

Her stomach was in *knots*.

It was a *hair-raising* experience.

That excuse left me with a *bad taste*.

I *see* your point.

I don't quite *grasp* your point.

They *hot-footed* it out of there.

I'd do it in a *heartbeat*.

What other examples can you add to this list? What metaphors would you use to convey the opposite of the ideas presented in each of the sentences above?

Basic Idea

Body-based metaphors are all around us. They are so common that some are called "dead." For example, we say "I see" or "I hear you" to convey understanding (though not necessarily agreement) without thinking about actually looking at something or hearing something. But even when metaphors have become automatic speech, they can still have an influence. Just think about how much worse a movie sounds if someone says "It stinks" rather than "It's bad." "Stink" is more powerful than "bad."

So What?

People influence us with their metaphors all the time. It is important to be on the lookout for them. They shape our viewpoints, whether or not we buy their argument or goods and services, pay attention to their displays, and have our imaginations fired up. You get the point. Of course, we employ metaphors, too, whether or not we are trying to sway someone by giving them a piece of our mind or trying to put their mind at rest. In short, metaphors are basic power tools for manipulating minds. You and I are sometimes their victims and sometimes their beneficiaries. Sometimes we are the fish and sometimes the fisherman.

Metaphors & Problem Solving

Introduction

Not only can metaphors give us a direct sense of someone or something through comparison (as with John and the ox in Think Key 33), they can also affect how we understand a problem and respond to it with solutions.

Exercise

Consider the two scenarios below. They are adapted from a well-known experiment. Note: If you are undertaking this exercise with someone else, it is suggested that one of you respond only to option A and the other person only to option B.

Option A.

Assume you are a state legislator reading a report about dramatic increases in crimes of all types in your state. The statistics in the report are quite disturbing, even gloomy. The crime rate is way up. The number of victims is way up as well. And the human suffering and property damage caused by crimes is also way, way up. The report you are reading calls for a war on crime. It speaks with alarm about criminals being beasts that prey on unsuspecting victims, often inflicting violence. It also stresses the need to be aggressive in hunting down and catching criminals to prevent further attacks on innocent people.

You are going to propose legislation to help address the crime issue. What are two or three of the measures you would be sure to include in your legislation? List them here:

1. _____
   _____
   _____

2. _____
   _____
   _____

3. _____
   _____
   _____

Option B.

Assume you are a state legislator reading a report about dramatic increases in crimes of all types in your state. The statistics in the report are quite disturbing, even gloomy. The crime rate is way up. The number of victims is way up as well.

And the human suffering and property damage caused by crimes is also way, way up. The report calls for taking serious action to contain the virus of crime infecting the state. The report stresses the need to stop this contagious outbreak of crime from becoming an epidemic and spreading throughout the state.

You are going to propose legislation to help address the epidemic of crime. What are two or three of the measures you would be sure to include in your legislation? List them here:

1. _____
   _____
   _____

2. _____
   _____
   _____

3. _____
   _____
   _____

Let's compare your recommendations with those of another group and see if your recommendations for A or B are similar to theirs. These are presented next.

Basic Idea

In a carefully designed experiment, people were asked to respond to a more complete report along the lines of Option A, in which crime was characterized as a warring beast. These people tended to suggest strong measures intended to scare, catch, and jail criminals and punish them with long prison sentences.

Another group, very similar to the people in the first group, responded to a report much like Option B. This report contained the exact same statistics as the first report, but characterized crime as a contagious virus. People in this group tended to suggest measures that address the root causes of crime. These measures were thought to help "inoculate" people against becoming criminals in the first place. They proposed antipoverty measures and education, employment, counseling, and after-school programs.

So What?

How information is presented or framed can dramatically alter how we respond to it. Lawyers presenting their cases to juries know this and use specialists in framing to help them help their clients. In the example above, people in each group were presented with the same information, but in one instance it was framed as a war or a battle, whereas In the other instance, it was framed as a contagious disease. The different metaphors elicited very different responses to the problem of crime.

We don't know from the study how aware participants were of the metaphors being used and their impact. Probably not very aware. When asked to justify their recommendations, participants used the statistics presented in the report, which were identical in the both versions. They didn't talk about crime as war or as a contagious disease. Those frames apparently exerted their influence below awareness.

Further Reading
Paul H. Thibodeau and Leah Boroditsky, "Metaphors We Think With: The Role of Metaphor in Reasoning," *PloS One* 6, no. 2 (February 2011).

Your Notes & Ideas

Embodied Cognition:
The Body in Mind

36

Bodily Experience & Judgment

Introduction

Sometimes, the connections between our mind and our body are so powerful that metaphorical verbal expressions are not needed to highlight the connection. Our bodily experiences literally shape our thinking and consequently our actions. Put differently, our bodies and minds are integrated like the ingredients making up a cake. Let's explore this in the following examples.

Exercise

Please respond to each item below. Simply circle or note your answer in some way. Your answer should be your best guess about how you think most people would respond. If you think you might respond differently from most people, make a note of this, too.

1. When people are stressed out, are they more likely or less likely to do such things as wash their car, do their laundry, organize their desk or bedroom, and make to-do lists than they are when they're relaxed?

   a. More likely to do these things

   b. Less likely to do these things

2. A group of people are asked to rank 10 music CDs in order of preference. They are then given as a gift a CD they ranked in the middle, say with a 5 or 6. Later, after doing something unrelated (called a distraction task), half of these people are asked to test a new soap by washing their hands with it. The other half are not asked to do this. Finally, the entire group is asked if they want to change their initial ranking of the gift CD.

   a. Did most people who washed their hands change their ranking of the gift CD?

   Circle one: Yes   No

   b. Did most people who did not wash their hands change their ranking of the gift CD?

   Circle one: Yes   No

3. People were asked to hold someone else's coffee for a short time. Some were asked to hold a very warm cup of coffee, and others were asked to hold an iced coffee. After they

returned the coffee to its owner, they listened to a description of a third person and were asked to characterize this person's personality. The description read to them was identical regardless of the coffee they held.

Were the people who held the warm cup of coffee more likely or less likely than those who held the iced coffee to say the person described had a warm personality?

a. More likely

b. Less likely

4. Some people were asked to think of a morally bad action. Other people were asked to think of a virtuous action. Everyone then drank what was determined by experts to be a neutral-tasting beverage.

a. How did the people who thought of a morally bad action rate the beverage? (Circle one)

i. Unfavorably   ii. Neutrally   iii. Favorably

b. How did the people who thought of a virtuous action rate the beverage? (Circle one)

i. Unfavorably   ii. Neutrally   iii. Favorably

Last question coming up.

5. There are four groups of people in this example. First, the liars. They are of two types. One is asked to write down a lie. Let's call them pencil liars. Another group is asked to say a lie out loud. Let's call them mouth liars.

Next are the truth tellers. They are also of two types. One group is asked to say something truthful out loud. We'll call them true mouths. Another group of truth tellers are asked write down a truth. We'll call them true pencils.

Okay, so far, we've got pencil liars and mouth liars. And we've got true mouths and true pencils.

After everyone has either written or told a lie or written or told a truth, they get to choose a gift for participating in the exercise. The gifts include mouthwash and hand soap, among other things.

Which one group chose the mouthwash gift more than did any other group?

A. Pencil liars

B. Mouth liars

C. True mouths

D. True pencils

Which one group chose hand soap more than did any other group?

A. Pencil liars

B. Mouth liars

C. True mouths

D. True pencils

We'll discuss other people's answers on the next page.

Basic Idea

We tend to make distinctions between mental states and physical states. This is partly because mental states are less easily observed than physical states. However, the distinction is a false one: the two are inextricably connected. Mental stress, for instance, can manifest itself as a stomachache or a headache. Conversely, pain from a pulled muscle or a burn can lead to mental stress. We demonstrate instinctive awareness of this fact when we let mental stress lead us to a flurry of activity—maybe doing the laundry or cleaning a room—that may defuse the stress. Meditation is an example of a physical activity consciously undertaken to defuse stress.

Now, how do your responses to the questions above compare with others such as those participating in the experiments? Let's begin with question 1. Most people responding to this question said that people who are stressed are more likely to engage in activities such as washing their car or making to-do lists than people who aren't stressed. People who answered this way may have reasoned as follows: stress often arises from things people can't control, so it can be soothing to engage in tasks that can be controlled. Other research supports this explanation. Also, as noted above, stress can be relieved through physical activity, so in the case of physical activities such as car washing, the activity may be a way of lessening the stress.

In question 2, people who washed their hands did tend to rerank the gift CD, and they ranked it much higher the second time. It was as if they were getting a fresh or clean start. Those who didn't wash their hands did not for the most part change their ranking. They didn't get a clean start for the task.

In question 3, people who held the warm cup of coffee tended to say the person being described to them had a warm personality. And, you guessed it, those who held the iced coffee described this person as having a cold personality. The physical sensation of heat or cold appears to have unconsciously influenced the judgment of a stranger's personality.

In question 4, a neutral-tasting beverage was found to be unpleasant and given an unfavorable rating by people who had been thinking of a morally bad action. By contrast, those who thought of a virtuous act gave the same beverage a favorable rating. Here again a state of mind set up by thinking about immoral or moral actions creates a mental disposition to experience a supposedly neutral beverage as either unpleasant or pleasant tasting.

Finally, pencil liars were more likely than any other group to choose hand soap from a set of gifts. It is as if washing their hands would distance them from having written a lie. Similarly, those saying a lie out loud were most likely to choose mouthwash as a gift. It is as if something repugnant still lingered in their mouths, which they wanted to expel with mouthwash. True mouths and true pencils didn't choose either the hand soap or mouthwash any more frequently than they picked other gifts.

A connection exists between our bodily experience and our mental judgments. In some cases, a connection is obvious—like when we put on a sweater because the temperature has dropped and we're feeling chilly. But here we're talking about connections that aren't obvious, times when our bodily experiences have more subtle, invisible influences on our thoughts. Washing our hands appears to help us cope with having written down a lie, and rinsing our mouths can help us cope with having told a lie. Holding a warm or cold cup of coffee can predispose us to describe someone's personality as warm or cold independent of the apparent facts.

So What?

What significance does this mind-body connection have in society? A big one. Consider the connection between being hungry or fatigued when making important decisions: studies found that how likely a parole review board was to grant paroles correlated with how close they were to a lunch or coffee break. Appeals that the board heard just before a coffee or lunch break had a much lower chance of success. Similarly, judges imposed harsher sentences as they approached a break. Their physical discomfort or need for sustenance just prior to a break or a meal affected their decisions. In these studies, the objective merit of the cases were no different throughout the day. Of course, the parole boards and judges were not aware of how their bodily needs for a break were affecting their judgments.

Elsewhere it has been found that students taking lecture notes on a laptop do more poorly on tests than do students who take notes longhand. It's hypothesized that the act of physically writing out notes, rather than typing them, requires more synthesis and reflection, which results in greater internalization of ideas. It is as if the laptop siphons the information away from the mind and it goes directly from ears to fingers.

Further Reading

Luca Cian, "Verticality and Conceptual Metaphors: A Systematic Review," *Journal of the Association for Consumer Research* 2, No. 4 (October 2017). The entire issue of this journal is devoted to embodied cognition.

Antonio Damasio, *The Strange Order of Things: Life, Feeling, and the Making of Cultures* (New York: Pantheon, 2018).

Mark Johnson, *The Body in the Mind: The Bodily Basis of Meaning, Imagination, and Reason* (Chicago: University of Chicago Press, 1987).

George Lakoff and Mark Johnson, *Philosophy in the Flesh: The Embodied Mind and Its Challenge to Western Thought* (New York: Basic Books, 1999).

Pam A. Mueller and Daniel M. Oppenheimer, "The Pen Is Mightier Than the Keyboard: Advantages of Longhand over Laptop Note Taking," *Psychological Science* 25, no. 6 (April 2014).

Embodied Cognition
Think Key | **37** | # Making Sense

Introduction

Our senses are accustomed to working together. We often coordinate them unconsciously. When they are working together to convey an experience, they magnify and reinforce one another, and the experience has greater impact. Senses, of course, are often a source of metaphor and influence us in that way, too.

Exercise

Please answer the following two questions before discussing them with other people.

> **Question 1.** Which is louder, sweet or sour?
>
> **Question 2.** Which is brighter, a sneeze or a cough?

Done? Okay, make a note of your answers and then let's see how they compare with answers other people give.

First, I'm sure you agree that the two questions are silly. Absolute nonsense. Clearly, there is no right answer to either one, and I'm sure you've never heard them before.

Second, that is not all you and others agree on. You also agree on the specific answers! I have posed these same baffling questions in speeches and other settings to thousands of people. Almost always they give the same answers.

Most people say sour is louder and a sneeze is brighter.

Let's add one more question for good measure.

Question 3. Look at the two shapes below. Which one is called Wooba and which is called Kiki?

Oh! And one more to help make the point: which shape would you expect to see on the label of a bottle of carbonated water, and which one on the label of a bottle of plain mineral water?

You probably gave the name Kiki to the sharp-pointed shape on the left and Wooba to the rounded shape on the right. Nearly everyone does, at least in English-speaking countries. And you likely assigned the one on the left to the label of the bottle of carbonated water and the one on the right to the mineral water. Correct?

Basic Idea

Why do very different people have the same answer to such silly questions? There should only be a fifty-fifty chance for a given answer.

Before addressing this question I am going to make a guess: for each question, most of you experienced your answer first—it suddenly came to mind—and only after that did you think of reasons why. That is what most people report. This illustrates some important things about our minds, including the following:

- We are sensemaking creatures. We latch onto a few cues—sometimes even just one—and make up a story. This is how gossip develops and how great novels are written. It doesn't take much effort to explain why our homework didn't get turned in or why we missed a deadline at work. We constantly make sense of things—come up with answers—even if a correct or meaningful answer doesn't exist.

- Our reasons for an action or thought are often found or created *after* decisions are made. We decide sour is louder before generating a reason why. And we may firmly believe our answer even if we can't explain it.

- Finally, different senses often work together to give us a full experience. Soft sounds go with round visual shapes. Dramatic sounds go with scary situations. Remember the famous sound track from the movie *Jaws* that caused us to imagine a shark? Apparently, the shark machine was broken when they had to film two men sitting on the edge of a dock at night. The producers created a musical score that would cause viewers to imagine something ominous—like a shark moving through the water. Moviegoers were likely more frightened by the score than they would have been had they seen the mechanical shark in action.

While your answers may be identical to other people's, your explanations for your answers—your stories—likely differ somewhat. However, one explanation as to why sour is louder is that in the English language the interior of our mouth takes on a similar shape when we pronounce both words. This apparently happens even when we think them silently. An explanation I sometimes receive for why a sneeze is brighter is that it is more explosive than a cough and explosions can be bright. Kiki has harsh sounds that go with the sharp spikes while Wooba has soft sounds that go with the rounded extensions.

So What?

We learn a great deal from our environment without knowing it. And because we share so much of this environment, such as a common language or set of laws, with strangers, we end up thinking a lot like other people we've never met. This explains in part how fads start and why some blogs catch on and others don't. We're kind of like a flock of birds dipping and turning all at exactly the same time.

38 | Being *Sense*-able

Introduction

The next two Think Keys follow a different avenue in exploring how we think. As a warm-up for them, I'd like to involve you in a step used in a special interview process. The process is called the "Zaltman metaphor elicitation technique," or ZMET for short. Many thousands of people around the world have been interviewed using the process and have engaged in variations of this particular step. The topics for the interviews are nearly as varied as the people and countries involved. Just one person at a time is interviewed—no groups—and the interview takes between 90 minutes and two hours.

Exercise

Just to be clear, there is no one common, specific answer to these questions. The questions used in this example, from a project sponsored by the World Bank, were asked of youth from different countries.

Please write down your answers. Let's begin.

1. A. When you think about the future, what *odor* (or smell or fragrance) comes to mind? That is, what odor would the future have, if it had one?

_____

  B. What odor would it *not* be like?

_____

2. A. When you think about the future, what *touch* comes to mind? What would its touch be like?

_____

  B. What touch would it *not* be like?

_____

3. A. What is the *sound* of the future?

_____

  B. What is *not* the sound of the future?

_____

Okay. We'll stop here. Ordinarily we'd continue with other senses. These questions are easy and even fun to ask. However, as you might guess, people respond with a strange look at first, almost as if they didn't hear the question correctly. But after a short hesitation they plunge ahead with meaningful answers.

Importantly, people are also asked to elaborate on their answers. For instance, "*Why* does the future taste like dirty water" and "*Why* it is not the taste of coffee?"

Basic Idea

We all know that we use our brains to think. But how do our brains do this job? If you answered, "In lots and lots of ways!" you'd be correct. But that doesn't get into the interesting nitty-gritty. One thing our brains depend on is input from our senses. Our senses help us grasp, understand, and get around in the world. They bring information to us, and they help us figure out what the information means. They also help us decide what to do with that information. So, it should not be a surprise that we can use our senses metaphorically to help us explain our ideas and experiences. The taste of coffee may not have bearing on the future, but our experience of that taste may be a great way to explain our expectations of the future.

So What?

Your senses are part of how you think. Not only are they information-gathering tools, but they also provide ways of expressing your thoughts and thus help shape those thoughts. In the World Bank project, the touch of the future was described like rough sandpaper, a scraped knee, getting a splinter in your foot, or putting on a frozen glove. These metaphors were chosen by the youth interviewed to help get across just how unpleasant and hurtful they thought the future might be.

To double-check the validity of sensory thoughts, it is important to ask what is *not* how the future will be. These youth made their worries clear by asserting that the future will not be the reassuring and optimistic touch of warm bread, hot tea, a down-filled bed, or a silk blouse. We learned in vivid, concrete ways just how anxious and even fearful these interviewees were about their future. Allowing them to think in terms of sensory images added power that abstract words like "anxious" and "pessimistic" alone fail to capture. (It should be noted that there were other interviewees who used more upbeat examples when describing how they thought the future would be.)

To understand our own and others' thinking we need to be attentive to the sensory metaphors used to express ideas. These reveal important, often unconscious, nuances about what people really think and feel.

Introduction

In addition to using sensory and body-based metaphors, we frequently use spatial language figuratively. For instance, we say we want to *get ahead* in life, or we describe a project as *forward looking* or public policy as *backward*, or we say that things are *looking up* or complain that someone is a real *downer*. We sometimes *fall behind* in class, get in *over our head*, are *on top* of things, *up front* about what we are thinking, and so on.

Exercise

There is a business office right next door to where you work. Below is a graph of the average amount of paper used by that business over time. As you can see, there is a constant increase over time except for the very last report. Place an X where you think the next X will appear when your next-door neighbor provides their next report on paper use.

it will be a cup of coffee and maybe some nuts or even potato chips.

Back? Now take a look at the graph below. It is an exact reproduction of the one to the left. This time, however, it involves an office located quite far away from you. Let's say the other side of the world. It is that office's report of its paper use over time.

Marked it down? Good. Before proceeding let's take a short break. Maybe a snack break. For me

As you can see, there is a constant increase over time except for the very last report. Where do you think the X will be the next time they report?

Place an X where you think it will appear when this distant office submits it next report on paper use.

Now look at the graph below. This shows where most people placed their X for the office right next door.

Yes, most people gave extra attention to the last report by their office neighbor. Did you?

Now for the surprise. When people (a separate but equivalent group of individuals who had not participated in the first part of the exercise—the part before you took a break) are told the graph is from an office on the other side of the world, not right next door, their guess about that office's paper consumption looks like this:

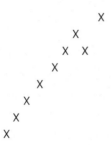

How about your guess? You may have been swayed by your decision regarding the office next door. But if you had not first thought of a nearby office—if, like the participants in the second part of this experiment, you were asked *only* about an office far away—there's a high likelihood you would have given more weight to the general upward trend in the reports and not been influenced by the outlying last report. That is, you would likely have placed an X indicating a continued overall increase in the use of paper.

Basic Idea

What appears to be going on is that people view information differently depending on whether the office involved is physically very near to them or very far away. People who were told that the office was far away saw the dip in the last reported use of paper as an exception; they gave more weight to the overall upward pattern in paper use. We can say they looked at the big picture. People who were told the data came from an office near to them gave greater weight to the last report and decided it was the start of a new, downward pattern. They weren't focused on the big picture but on that last data point—opposite interpretations of the same data apparently based on physical nearness/distance of the office involved.

So What?

The evidence we pay most and least attention to can be influenced by our physical proximity to the person, group, or object we are thinking about. Close physical proximity can translate into paying more attention—giving more weight—to the most recent or current information. This can result in what we've seen here: differing predictions based on an identical body of evidence depending on whether the evidence pertains to a person or group situated nearby or far away. Similarly, information about people in need in one's own community may be thought about differently—likely with more urgency—than information about people described in exactly the same way but located in a distant country.

Your Notes & Ideas

PART III

Moving Forward

Chapter Three
Commencement Time

Unlocked has started you on an important lifelong task: nurturing your mind. It's a task that deserves your full attention and is best accomplished by creating a safe space for trying out new exercises and ideas about your thinking. I call this space a "thought spot." It is both physical and attitudinal. It's a comfortable, disapproval-free setting that encourages reflection as you explore and perhaps go beyond your habitual thinking boundaries.

Creating a Thought Spot

A colleague, Bianca Philippi, who has years of experience in highly challenging public-school settings, provides this very practical advice for undertaking exercises such as the Think Keys:

> Doing the exercises outside in a natural setting or in a quiet, comfortable place indoors would be very helpful. There should not be loud sounds, vocal music or talking/shouting, TV, etc. ... or allowing the distraction or interruption of checking text messages or Instagram posts of friends. Cell phones should be put away and turned off while doing these exercises.

Our surroundings do matter. A crowded subway train is not a good choice for beginning an exploration of the mind, whereas sitting in a favorite chair with a favorite beverage likely is. Thought spot settings will vary, of course, depending on whether you are at work, at school, or at home.

But thought spots are more than physical settings. We have all studied and worked both in settings that encouraged free thinking and ones that definitely did not. My own experiences—of both types of environment—taught me things regarding attitudes and outlooks that helped me create thought spots when working with my own students, colleagues, and clients. I offer my insights below to help you create your own thought spots. These will be unique to you. The elements you include may vary depending on whether you're working solo or with others.

I want to acknowledge, however, that adopting these attitudes is easier said than done. It's like New Year's resolutions: although they're usually made with the sincere expectation of keeping them, we typically end up not keeping even the most realistic of them, and the same goes for adopting and practicing attitudes that help create a thought spot.

Boldness. You should feel safe in a thought spot, so be bold! Dare to change and dare to be different. Don't be afraid to depart from the familiar and try new ideas and practices. Have the courage to risk being wrong and the wisdom to learn from errors.

You can practice boldness by experimenting with something that's not a permanent commitment—something minor. In fact, you might play it out in your mind by imagining both good and bad outcomes of thinking differently. Then adjust the change to make a good outcome more certain. For instance, if you are challenging an assumption, think about what challenge would elicit "That's interesting!" as a response from yourself or from others instead of "That's obvious" or "That's absurd." This middle-ground challenge is more inviting to others and more motivating to engage yourself. Be sure, too, to reflect on what evidence from independent sources is available to support and to critique your challenge.

Continuous Pursuit of Excellence. "Okay" Isn't good enough. Constantly scan your environment for better thinking options. Don't let contentment with current thinking become your cage. In looking for better ways to think, ask other people how they generate interesting ideas. Some people describe special settings. (Yes, "in the shower" often comes up.) Some will describe something they've read, perhaps a biography or an editorial. Others will describe accidental or serendipitous events. Those last ones in particular require a receptive mind, one willing to listen. So periodically ask yourself, "Am I listening with an open mind? Am I inadvertently closing off another way of thinking about topic X?" If you haven't recently heard a very different way of thinking about that topic, then perhaps you are not listening well. Many new product ideas are encountered in research on an unrelated product, because the researchers or managers are not caged in by an immediate task. They have an outlook that asks, "How can what I am learning about Febreze be applied to product development in other areas? Does this information illuminate a consumer need we haven't encountered before?"

Passionate Curiosity. Always wonder why. Current thinking has its own gravity field. Achieving escape velocity isn't easy. Idle curiosity alone won't propel you, but passionate curiosity will. Passion comes from treating as close and trusted friends the questions and perspectives you've encountered in *Unlocked*.

A graduate-school friend earned the nickname, "Who Who What What." He was always asking questions. He still does. No surprise, then, that he became a leader in one of the world's most successful companies. A characteristic of wonderers, be they carpenters, chefs, investment bankers, architects, or machine operators, is the ability to formulate an important question. While most people focus on answers, wonderers focus on questions. Good thing, too: if weren't for questions, where would answers be? The quality of a question directly affects the value of an answer. I encourage you to wonder most about what you understand least concerning a problem or task. For instance, the most successful advertising programs, like those from Kimberly-Clark, Coca-Cola, Frito-Lay, and Whirlpool, are ones whose underlying market research answers questions about what managers know least about consumers. In contrast, ineffective programs are based on superficial questions confirming answers that may already exist.

Empathy. Walk in another's shoes. Sometimes a thinking task requires you to imagine being another person, or at least being in their situation. This requires understanding or reading others' feelings. It doesn't require you to agree with them. If you explore your thinking with other people in a group (something I recommend), try hard to understand and respect their personal history, thoughts, feelings, and values. And they need to do the same for you.

Learning how others think has at least two benefits. First, it may uncover a way of thinking previously hidden to you, a way of seeing things you hadn't considered before. It may suggest a change you might dare to make, yourself, as an experiment. I once participated in a conference where invitees were required to coauthor a thought piece with someone whom they believed thought entirely differently from them. My coauthor and I very quickly found one another. We shared the same values but had very different ways of enacting them. The result was an essay I am very proud of, and the experience greatly impacted my thinking.

Intellectual Devotion. Seek what's next. Intellectual devotion is a commitment to continued learning about how you think. It arises from passionate curiosity, the pursuit of excellence, and a belief that how you think shapes the quality of your thoughts and life. Intellectual devotion requires you to be untiring in your search for ways to nurture your mind.

Intellectual devotion, like many habits, requires effort to put in place, but once in place, it runs on autopilot. Sometimes you'll find yourself trying out something new in private to avoid the risk of looking foolish to others. Other times you will actively share how you think with others to gain

their perspectives. Today we have elaborate yet convenient ways of accessing, testing, and sharing diverse ways of thinking. Be an active participant in these systems. You owe it to yourself.

Summing Up

Your interactions with the various Think Keys have equipped you to continue improving how you think on your own. You can find more Think Keys on **geraldzaltman.com/unlocked**. Additionally, I strongly encourage you to find or develop similar thought-provoking challenges on your own. (I hope you will consider sharing those.)

Finally, in the first chapter, I shared a collage representing what I hoped your mind's eye might see as you reflect on your experience with this book. I said that while your own vision would not resemble mine in the particulars, I hoped and suspected that the meanings of our images would overlap. Now might be a good time to pause and create an image that expresses your experience with *Unlocked*. And I'd love to learn about it. (**unlocked@geraldzaltman.com**)

Acknowledgements

With the benefit of hindsight, it is evident this project began long ago. As a result, there are many people and programs whose fingerprints are present throughout *Unlocked*. These contributors are too numerous to acknowledge individually but mention can be made of settings in which I've been privileged to benefit from their ideas. First are the scholars from diverse disciplines whose works this book builds upon. Most go uncited as citation would produce yet another book. Next are colleagues at Olson Zaltman, a market and organizational research and consulting firm, whose dedication to the values discussed in Chapter Three have inspired me. In addition, I have learned considerably from many of Olson Zaltman's clients.

Shortly after joining Harvard University I was invited to participate in a university-wide interdisciplinary program called the Mind Brain Behavior Interfaculty Initiative. This program provided one of the most impactful learning experiences of my career. It also led to my establishing the Mind of the Market Lab at the Harvard Business School with cognitive psychologist Stephen M. Kosslyn, PhD, (founding dean and chief academic officer of the Minerva Schools at the Keck Graduate Institute). This, too, had great impact on this book. I am grateful to Dr. Kosslyn, the Lab's corporate sponsors, and the Harvard Business School's Division of Research, which is a source of continuing support. Particular thanks to Jan Rivkin, PhD, senior associate dean for research, for his encouragement with this book. I must also acknowledge the support of literally hundreds of HBS graduate students and participants in executive education programs who allowed me to engage their minds and who returned the favor. Among other things, they taught me that being a teacher is the best way to remain a student.

Many others have made unique contributions to this book and have made it better by sharing their professional experiences and insights. They are: Vincent Barabba (Market Insight Corporation), Lewis Carbone (Experience Engineering), Robin Coulter, PhD, (University of Connecticut), Nancy Cox (Hallmark Cards), Diana-Luiza Dumitriu, PhD, (National School of Political Studies and Public Administration, Romania), James Forr (Olson Zaltman), Stephen Haeckel (IBM), Pamela Holland, Nick Kimminau, Kathryn LaTour, PhD, (Cornell University), Ralph Linsalata (Media Advisory Partners), Gary Massel, PhD, Lynn Massel, Horace P. Maxcy, PhD, (educational consultant), Joseph Meth, Jerry Olson (Olson Zaltman), Bianca Philippi (UCLA and Creative Insights), Nicole Raynard, William Totten, Michael Voncannon, Manjit Yadav, PhD, (Texas A&M University), and Lindsay Zaltman (Olson Zaltman).

I am especially fortunate in receiving support from people who have unique communication skills and familiarity with the behavioral sciences. In alphabetical order, Kathleen Fleury (editor in chief, *Down East* Magazine) brought to bear a keen eye from her past and current editorial experiences. She often forced me to rethink a position or direction and displayed a canny knack for asking key questions. Francesca Forrest, an accomplished author in her own right, provided detailed comment on the book's exposition. In the process she displayed her own sharp intellect with perceptive critique of many ideas and examples. The book is immeasurably better because of their contributions. Both Kathleen and Francesca made sure I practiced what I preach in the book's exercises. Luz Velazquez (staff assistant, Harvard Business School) performed the Herculean task of finding the countless background documents relevant to the ideas advanced here. Her persistent sleuthing in the published literature is greatly appreciated.

When all is said and done, the presentation of material matters a great deal. In my previous books, designers were always invisible to me. Not so this time. I consider myself very fortunate to have worked with Kathryn Massel (DZYN, LLC). She has a wonderful sense of how a book's contents greet the eye and how that shapes our involvement with it.

These acknowledgements should make clear how fortunate I am in having the support of so many fine and varied people. Some of those mentioned, directly or indirectly, will know there is one other person who has provided invaluable support: my wife, Ann Gove Zaltman. She has patiently read and reread numerous drafts of the book, brought ideas to my attention, actively engaged in group sessions testing Think Keys, and tolerated my frequent absences while reading and writing. This book would ordinarily be dedicated to Ann if it weren't for one other party to the book, my grandchildren. As explained in the Preface, they too played a role in the genesis of *Unlocked*.

About the Author

Gerald Zaltman is the Joseph C. Wilson Professor of Business Administration Emeritus at the Harvard Business School (HBS). He was codirector of HBS's Mind of the Market Laboratory and a cofounder of the research-based consulting firm Olson Zaltman Associates, whose clients include some of the world's most respected firms. Olson Zaltman Associates has worked in nearly 40 countries developing deep insights about consumer behavior. Professor Zaltman holds a PhD in sociology from the Johns Hopkins University, an MBA from the University of Chicago, and a BA from Bates College.

His interests focus on customer behavior and marketing strategy. His best-selling book *How Customers Think: Essential Insights into the Mind of the Market* (2003) has been translated into 20 languages. *Marketing Metaphoria: What Deep Metaphors Reveal about the Minds of Consumers* (2008), written with Lindsay Zaltman, has also been published in multiple languages. It addresses the unconscious frames that influence consumer and manager thought and behavior. And Professor Zaltman has written numerous other books on social change, research, and thinking.

Professor Zaltman's work has been featured in the *New York Times, Fortune, Forbes, U.S. News & World Report, Time, Fast Company, American Demographics,* and other major publications. Professor Zaltman is a consultant to corporations around the globe and frequent keynote speaker at major conferences. He has received three patents for market research tools. One patented technique, ZMET, is used around the world by major firms and international agencies.

Professor Zaltman received the biannual Sheth Foundation Gold Medal Award for Exceptional Contributions to Marketing Scholarship and Practice. He was inducted into the inaugural American Marketing Association's Fellow Program recognizing members who have made significant contributions to the research, theory, and practice of marketing. Other awards include the American Marketing Association's Richard D. Irwin Distinguished Marketing Educator Award in 1989, the Association for Consumer Research Distinguished Fellow Award in 1990, the Knowledge Utilization Society's Thomas J. Kiresuk Award for Excellence in Scientific Research in 1992, the JAI Press Distinguished Scholar Award from the Society for Marketing Advances in 2000, the ARF Member Recognition Award in 2007, and the Massachusetts Institute of Technology's Henry Grady "Buck" Weaver Award in 2008, sponsored by General Motors, for outstanding work in bringing knowledge and practice together. He is included in Sage Publications' "Legends in Marketing" series, which republished five volumes of his leading-edge works in 2018.

Made in the
USA
Columbia, SC